JEWISH BIBLE PERSONAGES IN THE NEW TESTAMENT

Norman M. Cohen

UNIVERSITY
PRESS OF
AMERICA

Lanham • New York • London

Copyright © 1989 by

University Press of America,® Inc.

4720 Boston Way
Lanham, MD 20706

3 Henrietta Street
London WC2E 8LU England

Library of Congress Cataloging-in-Publication Data

Cohen, Norman, M., 1950–
Jewish Bible personages in the New Testament / Norman M. Cohen.
p. cm.
Bibliography: p.
1. Jews in the New Testament. 2. Bible. N.T.—Relation to the
Old Testament. 3. Bible. N.T.—Criticism, Interpretation, etc. I. Title.
BS2545.J44C64   1988
225'.089924—dc 19   88–31249 CIP
ISBN 0–8191–7252–9 (alk. paper)

All University Press of America books are produced on acid-free paper.
The paper used in this publication meets the minimum requirements of American
National Standard for Information Sciences—Permanence of Paper for Printed Library
Materials, ANSI Z39.48–1984.   ∞

My heart was stirred to seek wisdom,
Therefore I have gained a good possession.
The Lord gave me a tongue as my reward,
And I will praise God with it.

Sirach 51:21-22

Acknowledgments

I wish to express my gratitude to the many people who have guided and encouraged me: my family, friends, and congregants for bearing with me throughout this endeavor; their patience, understanding and support seemed to me at times never ending.

The library staff of the Hebrew Union College-Jewish Institute of Religion, Cincinnati, without whom many of the resources and texts would not have been available to me.

Both congregations that I have served as rabbi have been ideal environments for my personal and professional development. I am indebted to K.K. Bene Israel/Rockdale Temple in Cincinnati and to Bet Shalom Congregation in Minneapolis for their confidence and faith in me.

I am grateful to my devoted and talented secretary Rita Lusky, who did a mammoth job of typing, to Sarah Jane Schwarzenberg, whose familiarity with the computer helped immeasurably in the word processing, and to Irv Steinfeldt, for his helpful editorial suggestions.

The faculty of the Hebrew Union College-Jewish Institute of Religion provided their advice in many areas. This is reflected in the numerous footnotes attributed to my teachers.

Rabbi Michael Cook, who, more than any other individual, guided and advised, coaxed and encouraged, challenged and questioned my work. His enthusiasm, discipline, expertise, sense of humor, and friendship are much appreciated.

Table of Contents

Tables

Introduction

Theological discussions between Christians and Jews are becoming more commonplace than ever before. Interfaith study groups and church/synagogue interreligious activities have helped Americans of different religious faiths get to know each other better and understand the similarities and differences that make us who we are.

Some of those discussions center around the Bible and what it means to each of us. When the word Bible itself is mentioned, it means one thing to Christians and quite another to Jews. In fact, one of the most common problems to overcome in interfaith theological discussions is the issue of vocabulary. While Christians feel quite comfortable calling the Jewish Bible the Old Testament, Jews do not. We can simply say Jewish Bible when referring to our Holy Scriptures or we can more appropriately call it the Tanakh (a Hebrew acronym for Jewish Scripture).

One aspect of Bible study is to examine the various Tanakhic personages that are the heroes and villains of the Biblical stories. However, there, too, we may encounter some difficulty. When Jews and Christians talk about such characters as Moses and Elijah, Abraham and Sarah, they often understand those people in very different ways. Jews see those personages not only as figures of the Bible, but as characters of our tradition, expanded upon in the Midrash, the great collections of Rabbinic interpretations. Similarly, Christians find a guide and influence to their understanding of these personages by the way in which many of them are mentioned or appear in the New Testament and in other church writings.

This book focuses on some of those specific differences and why those differences exist. With a better understanding of why our friends and neighbors value the Bible, we can expand our respect and share new perspectives with each other.

There have been many literary studies which have dealt with the New Testament's citation of Biblical passages, prophecies, and events. Some of these works have also touched upon the specific use of Tanakhic personages by New Testament writers. This book is an attempt to understand the exegetical and theological role assigned these personages and the implications of their use by New Testament authors.

Chapter I serves as an introduction by presenting a general overview of the relationship of the New Testament to the Jewish Bible. We have included a wide spectrum of scholarly opinions regarding that relationship.

Chapter II is a compilation of the 400 explicit references to Biblical personages found in New Testament writings. We attempt by the use of tables to indicate the frequency with which individual personages appear and the location of their appearances in New Testament writings.

Chapter III is a systematic examination of these explicit references as well as of suggested implicit references. The sequence of personages is arranged on the basis of decreasing frequency, beginning with Moses. Our aim is to elucidate their theological significance to the authors who employ them.

Chapter IV concludes our study with our personal reflections on the use of Tanakhic personages by the New Testament writers: its implications with regard to the general relationship of the New Testament and the Jewish Bible as well as the broader connection of Christianity and Judaism.

Although some studies have treated a few selected Tanakhic characters, a more exhaustive treatment achieving an overall perspective has been lacking. It is our hope that this book will help fill that void and provide the groundwork and incentive for further research in this area.

CHAPTER I

Introductory Considerations: The General Use of Scripture in the New Testament

The service concluded with the singing of a hymn. Phylacteries were stripped off. Several men picked up bags of tools and rushed off to their day's labor. The congregation disbanded quickly. Then the reader who had conducted the service approached Elisha. He was a kindly Jew, soft-spoken and respectful for all that he was unmistakably suspicious.

"To what, Master," he asked cautiously, "may we ascribe the honor of the attendance of so distinguished a guest?"

Elisha, always uncomfortable before deference, smiled shyly. "I am not present," he assured him, "as a member of the Sanhedrin. I merely wish information concerning the beliefs and practices of your group." . . .

The man (the reader) *smiled, gratefully.*

"Perhaps," he went on, "the Rabbi is interested in studying our faith for his own sake. He may have heard of our Savior and, like so many others, felt himself attracted to Him."

"Not exactly," Elisha corrected. "Right now I am merely seeking information. Most of all, I want to know on what your belief rests."

Without hesitation the Nazarene replied, "On Scripture, of course, which we revere as you do."

"On anything else as well?"

"Why yes, on the life and teaching of the Messiah also."

"And that is all?" Elisha asked, eagerly, reckless of the implications of his question.

"What more," the Nazarene replied, startled, "would the rabbi want than the fulfillment of the words of the prophets?"

This passage from Milton Steinberg's historical novel, <u>As A Driven Leaf</u>,[1] depicts Elisha ben Abuyah's visit to a first century gathering of Jewish Christians. In his search for truth and security, Elisha finds that these early Christian spokesmen place a paramount emphasis on Scripture.[2] They feel that Scripture is a firm foundation for their faith and they find Scripture's fulfillment in the life and teachings of Jesus.

This book is, in general, an examination of the relationship of the New Testament to the Bible and, in particular, of the exegetical and theological role assigned Biblical personages in New Testament writings. In preparation for this study, a number of fundamental questions must be posed and answered. What evidence is there of a relationship between the New Testament and Jewish Scriptures? What underlies this relationship? In what forms is this relationship manifested? Finally, did New Testament writers have direct recourse to Scripture itself or were they dependent on sources (i.e.., practical aids such as testimony books)?

Evidence of a Relationship between the New Testament and Jewish Scriptures

There is a wide spectrum of opinion on this question ranging, on the one hand, from those who claim that almost every line of New Testament is related to Scripture to those, on the other hand, who try to deny that dependence.

C. H. Dodd suggests that the reader underline various Scriptural texts that are used or referred to by New Testament writers. He predicts the results: certain portions of the Jewish Bible will be covered with pencil marks.[3] It is thus obvious that New Testament writers utilized Scripture, and that certain sections of the Bible were drawn upon to an especially great degree. Dodd does, however, caution against overspeculation, acknowledging that detailed study is necessary to verify that a particular New Testament writer actually used a particular Scriptural text.[4]

H. M. Shires' work, Finding the Old Testament in the New, indeed represents such a study. Shires states that "of the twenty-seven books of the N.T., only the one-chapter letter to Philemon shows no direct relationship to the O.T."[5] Shires' findings are well-documented with charts and tables of reference and parallels which demonstrate the close relationship of the New Testament and the Jewish Bible: "1604 New Testament passages . . . are directly dependent upon the Old Testament!"[6] Many other scholars agree that the New Testament manifests extensive dependence on the Bible, among them J. Jeremias,[7] A. G. Hebert,[8] E. D. Freed, [9] and G. von Rad.[10] The New Testament writers themselves would be the last to deny or disapprove of their usage of Scriptural texts.[11] Indeed, when in the second century, Marcion argued that Christianity disassociate itself from the Jewish Bible, his suggestion was deemed heretical.[12]

4

R. Gundry agrees that there is some usage of Scripture by New Testament writers but he shows much more restraint than Shires. He uses the argument "from absence" to reduce the number of instances in which the New Testament allegedly employed certain Scriptural elements. In his own words: "Had the tradition been erected upon the OT text, we would not have had the absence of elements in the OT text which were extremely suitable."[13] Gundry's argument explains that since the details from the Scriptures are fewer than we would expect in any given case of presumed dependence, the dependence is no longer to be presumed! Gundry thus accepts many Gospel episodes as completely credible, where others would suspect that Scriptural motifs have been employed; e.g. the incident of Jesus' riding on two animals is a case of a young donkey whose mother was allowed to accompany it to keep it quiet in the crowd;[14] it was not a case of misinterpretation of Zech. 9:9.[15]

A. T. Hanson advances an extreme view: not only is the reliance of New Testament on Scripture all-pervasive, but Jesus Christ is actually present in the Jewish Bible. Hanson's argument and illustrations will be dealt with later in this chapter.[16]

F. F. Bruce criticizes those scholars who go too far in reading New Testament into the Bible. He cites examples of scholars who find Jesus Christ wrestling with Jacob, and see the cross of Christ in Haman's gallows.[17]

R. V. G. Tasker is critical of the "new" approach to New Testament wherein scholars "overstate" the case, "to bring in rather fanciful solutions where quite ordinary and mundane considerations are sufficient to explain the narrative."[18] Some, for example, see the incident of the naked young man (Mk. 14:51-52) as dependent on Amos 2:16 ("And he that is courageous among the mighty shall flee away naked in that day, saith the Lord.") But the young man was Mark himself, so Tasker argues; there is no need for recourse to Amos! "Gospel criticism ought not to become a test of ingenuity in discovering the maximum number of possible Old Testament passages which may have some bearing as explanations for the order of incidents, or the manner in which they are described in the Gospels."[19]

5

The arguments of Dodd and Shires are the most convincing; we, too, contend that the New Testament relies heavily on Scriptural antecedents.

What Underlies the Relationship between the New Testament and Jewish Scriptures?

Why did the Bible loom so large for the New Testament writers? Perhaps, as Dodd suggests, it was merely a literary device.[20] Evidence from the Dead Sea tends to support this claim. "Recent researches in the Qumran scrolls have shown that in the NT period the interweaving of scriptural phraseology and one's own words was a conscious literary method."[21] Shires agrees that "the N.T. reveals much of this form of literary blending."[22]

Writers today often make reference to well-known classics of literature. For the New Testament writers, these classics were naturally less numerous. In fact, "for the N.T. writers, the O.T. was the best known body of literature of any then in existence."[23] Jesus and his earliest followers were Jews for whom Judaism and Scripture were essential. Since Christianity began as a Jewish sect, it is only natural that "the church from the beginning tied its teachings about Jesus closely to Scripture."[24]

Paul was directly responsible for parts of the New Testament and he influenced a good deal of the remainder. Paul, who was born and raised as a Jew, was himself "immersed in the content and teachings of the OT."[25] E. E. Ellis feels that it is nearly impossible to overstate the Bible's significance for Paul's theology.[26] Shires, too, recognizes that "Paul was influenced by his Jewish training."[27] Shires even believes that, "with one or two possible exceptions, all the writers of the N.T. were also Jews."[28] It becomes clear that Scripture was part of the heritage and background of most, if not all, New Testament writers, and hence potentially influential in any writing they produced.

It is only to be expected that Scripture would influence the New Testament since the latter itself aspired to be considered sacred. For New Testament writers, Christian writings were revelatory; and the employment of Scripture only served to underpin their authenticity.[29] Thus, the writer of the First Epistle of Peter already assumes that

Scriptural passages are applicable to Christ and the church.[30] This assumption became reinforced by the succession of Christian writers.

The New Testament showed an historical awareness that was absent from other writings of the day, such as most of those of Philo. Dodd contrasts Philo's flatness, his lack of historical perception, to that manifested by the New Testament writers.[31] Their sense of history naturally led them to allude to Christianity's own antecedents, as recorded in the Bible.

Jesus himself was said to mention Scriptural events: e.g., the Passover and the Exodus, also various personalities such as Abraham, Abel, Moses, etc. Underlying such allusions, Shires believes, is Jesus' own interest in the history of his people.[32] Christians recognized "no discontinuity between Jesus and the saving acts of the O.T."[33] for God's purpose was declared through Israel and Jesus served as the climax of the historical events depicted in Scripture; the Bible, accordingly, becomes as significant to Christians as it was to Jews.

Nor should we forget that the early disciples saw themselves as Israel, not the new Israel nor a sect within Israel. They were the real Israel, while those Jews who rejected Christ "forfeited their covenant."[34] If the New Testament is regarded only as a continuation of the work of the Biblical God, where then lies the uniqueness of Christianity? Shires concludes that it is found not in a completely new truth but in a full revelation of what was already revealed in the Bible. The New Testament alludes to a continuous revelation by God through its interpretation and application.[35]

Bruce maintains that the New Testament should at least be seen as a "sequel if not the sequel,"[36] as Vatican Council II suggests in its statement that "God, the inspirer and author of both Testaments, wisely arranged that the New Testament be hidden in the Old and the Old be made manifest in the New."[37] Dodd emphasizes that the Bible is the root of the New Testament, the rock from which it is hewn. He thinks that the Biblical influence and origin is much greater than its Hellenistic counterpart.[38] Dodd does not mean to minimize the role played by Hellenism in the development of the church and its writings but rather to explicate the fundamental role played by Jewish influences.

A. T. Hanson believes that the reason the New Testament is so inextricably related to the Jewish Scripture is the presence of Jesus Christ in both volumes, the Old as well as the New. Whereas typologists base their contentions on the appearance of "types" of Jesus in Scripture, Hanson contends: "one thing is certain: if Jesus was present in any event in Old Testament history, there can be no question of that event representing a type of Christ at the same place and time."[39] "Where Christ is present there is no room for the type of Christ."[40]

Hanson then sets out to show that the New Testament writers actually believed that Jesus appeared in Scripture, "that the pre-existent Jesus was actually present at certain points in Old Testament history."[41] Different names of God, such as Kyrios ("lord"), are intended as signals indicating Jesus' presence. Some of the situations in which Hanson suggests Jesus' presence are as the rock in Ex. 17,[42] and as the Spirit which spoke to Moses on Mount Sinai.[43] Hanson explains: "How Christ was the Rock is a question which we cannot stop to examine. It is probably as incapable of a full answer as is the precisely parallel question about the mode of Christ's presence in the Eucharist."[44] So also was Christ present with Moses on Sinai: ". . . in Paul's view Moses' motive in putting the veil on his face was to prevent the children of Israel seeing Christ."[45]

Hanson firmly believes that this was Paul's frame of reference when he composed his epistles. Paul believed it was possible to have faith in Christ during Moses' time.[46] When Isaiah chastises the Israelites for unbelief, Paul understands this to be Jesus speaking to the Jews. Since the Jews never stopped believing in "God, the Father," even after the incarnation of Jesus, then it must have been "God, the Son" in whom they did not believe.[47]

Closely related to the concept of historical continuity is that of prophecy fulfillment. "As the OT itself notes, the 'last word' is not in it but in the New Covenant which fulfills and supersedes it."[48] The New Testament writers were certainly convinced that theirs was this new covenant and in the course of their teachings would make reference to the Bible showing how Jesus and Christianity fulfill the Bible. The book of Acts has numerous examples of this practice, including 8:26-38, where Jesus is shown to be the fulfillment of the lamb reference of Isaiah 53:7-8, and 18:24-28, where Appolos refutes the Jews in public by showing that Jesus fulfills the Scriptures.[49]

Paul himself proved Jesus' authenticity by referring to Scriptural passages. He believed that Jesus was the Messiah, that he suffered and was resurrected because it was "according to the Scriptures". The use of this phrase gives significance to the New Testament events by showing that the Scriptural prophecies are fulfilled by them.[50]

Tasker would go one step further and say that the New Testament not only was the fulfillment but a supersedence, an upstaging effort. "Jesus' sacrifice on the cross achieved what the Jewish system of animal sacrifice, which foreshadowed it, had failed to achieve, namely, the reconciliation of sinful man to God."[51]

Some would argue that the Bible could not be appreciated without the New Testament, just as the opposite is true. In the same way that an understanding of Christ necessitates a familiarity with the fall of man, the faith of Abraham, and the giving of the Law via Moses, so too, an appreciation of the Bible requires its interpretation in the light of the New Testament. The Jews, according to Paul, read the Bible with veils over their minds, unable to see its real significance.[52] Although the Jew would disagree that the New Testament was the interpretation necessary to shed light on the Bible, history shows that midrashic interpretation was indeed necessary for "proper" Biblical understanding.

All of these explanations as outlined thus far really point to the question of authority, the one underlying reason for the usage of Scripture in the New Testament. We know that any good presentation or argument has a source of authority; authority is the cornerstone of any religious foundation and must be recognized as such by the people being addressed. In the case of the New Testament, that recognition was accorded to the Bible. As Dodd contends: "The Christian Gospel could not be adequately or convincingly set forth unless the communication of facts about Jesus was supported by references to the Old Testament."[53]

The early Christians were also concerned with taking their message to the gentiles of the Graeco-Roman world. The prestige of the Bible in the eyes of the gentiles was closely bound up with the Bible's antiquity. The age of a work or concept commanded great awe and respect on their part, so much so that Josephus describes Abraham as teaching mathematics and astronomy to the Egyptians in order to elicit respect from the gentiles for Abraham's expertise in these fields and for the credit due him for teaching the rest of the world.[54] Josephus even entitles his work <u>Antiquities of the Jews</u>. This approach to authority was probably understood as well by the early Christians who capitalized on it by using the Bible to evoke esteem from the gentiles. By associating their writings with Scripture, the early Christians were carrying themselves back to the beginning of the universe. It is likely that gentiles, including the so-called "God-fearers", were first exposed to this type of preaching when they attended addresses by Christian missionaries, such as Paul, to synagogue audiences.

Thus, there are many possible reasons for the use of Scripture by the New Testament writers: to serve as a popular literary device, to supply historical background, to provide a continuum of Jesus' presence in both Testaments, to demonstrate fulfillment of prophecy. Underlying all of these reasons is the key issue: authority.

In What Forms Is the Relationship Manifested?

The most obvious use of the Bible by New Testament writers is citation of its texts. Shires presents an explicit and thorough statistical summary of this type of usage.[55] For example, consider that "there are 260 chapters in the whole N.T., and only twelve of these contain no instance of a direct relationship of some form with the O.T. . . . . It can be quickly seen that 229 of the 260 chapters have in each at least two citations of or specific references to the O.T."[56] In many of the cases the quotations are preceded by an introductory formula,[57] while, in other cases, the quotations are merely inserted into the text. Sometimes the words are specifically attributed to one of the prophets rather than to the Bible in general. The specific identification of a text with a particular prophet is still, in essence, a general Biblical quotation as "the apparent attribution of Scripture to a human author may only be the writer's way of fixing the place of the O.T. citation."[58] When it says, "according to Isaiah", it might just as well

10

say, "according to the Bible." In some cases, the text is even attributed to the wrong prophet.

Another peculiarity of New Testament quotation of Bible is that often the quotation is inexact or wrongly attributed. Because the citations so often do not agree with either the Septuagint or the Hebrew text, we must assume that the words are from a text which is not extant and/or the writers were quoting from memory. Shires believes that the New Testament writers probably did not have a Bible in front of them as they wrote. He reminds us that they would have had the unenviable task of unrolling a long and unwieldy scroll each time they needed a reference. Still it is apparent that they knew the text well. "It is often very difficult to determine whether a passage taken from the O.T. is a quotation or an allusion."[59]

Ellis concurs: often the quotation came as a result of memory. But he points out that the reason for incongruities with the original text is due more to exegetical purpose or literary custom that to "memory lapse".[60]

Dodd suggests that the selection of Biblical quotations was not as important for the New Testament writers as the context from which they were chosen. Therefore, the exact wording is not as significant as the total picture which the quotation elicits. According to Gundry, "Dodd concludes that the NT authors were not engaged in searching through the OT for isolated proof texts, but that they exploited 'whole contexts selected as the varying expression of certain fundamental and permanent elements in the biblical revelation.'"[61]

Allusion, then, is the second major form which the New Testament employed in appropriating text from the Bible. If Dodd's theory is correct then allusion is exercised almost every time a quotation is cited.

Bruce, in The New Testament Development of Old Testament Themes, deals with the manner of expansion and allusion on such themes as God's rule, salvation, covenant and messiah, and of development of such themes as the Exodus, Jerusalem restored, and Paradise regained.[62] Students of Rabbinic literature know of similar thematic development among the Rabbis of the Midrash and Talmud. In fact, parts of the New Testament have been popularly labelled as midrash themselves. ". . . The first two chapters of the Gospels of Matthew and Luke are not to be considered historical, but as what the Jews call a midrash."[63]

The midrashic method is generally creative imaginative explanation of already known material. The term "midrash" is sometimes even used pejoratively to discredit a comment that is merely a personal biased interpretation and not fact-based. The interesting thing to note is that generally the Rabbis were very honest in their conviction that what they were expounding was also the word of God. It must be assumed that the New Testament writers were similarly motivated.

With all due respect, however, we must insist that, when literary allusions are utilized, they are done so with a particular bias, no matter who makes the selection. As Shires has written in regard to the New Testament writers, "Even as they are used, O.T. verses are changed and given new meanings."[64] In their literary allusions, it is extremely difficult, if not impossible, to determine the extent of Rabbinic influence on New Testament writers or vice versa. The problems of dating a particular Rabbinic text are only part of the general difficulty of determining the birth date of an idea. Just because an idea first appeared in a written text in 200 C.E. does not mean that the idea could not have been popular for two to three hundred years earlier. In fact, much of Jewish and Christian tradition began in an oral stage before being copied down.

Scholars hold varying opinions with regard to the dependence either of New Testament writers on the Rabbis or the opposite. Ellis typifies one prevalent approach when he claims that, although Paul has some messianic references that parallel those of the Rabbis, for the most part he bases his messianic writings on his exegesis as a Christian.[65] The possibility of some interdependence is not nearly as significant as the fact that both the Rabbis and the New Testament writers used literary allusion as one of their forms in expounding the Bible.

Most scholars feel that the New Testament does not employ an allegorical use of Scripture to any meaningful degree. There are, however, two clear-cut examples, as Dodd points out: in Galatians 4:21-31, where Hagar, Ishmael, Sarah, and Isaac are used in depicting the displacement of Israel by the Christians as the new people of God, the new chosen son; and in Hebrews 7:1-10, where Melchizedek serves as the priest-king-prophet.[66] Ellis would be quick to agree that the former is the Pauline text most often compared with Philonic allegorical exegesis.[67] Nevertheless, both scholars would strenuously oppose any exaggeration of the extent of New Testament use of allegory. Ellis insists that Paul, for example, uses typology much more extensively than allegory which, by contrast, actually receives very minor emphasis.[68]

Dodd's denial of allegory as a dominant form in New Testament writing is based on his claim, explained earlier, of the New Testament awareness of history.[69] Allegory ignores history by fantasizing the characters employed therein. For the historically conscious New Testament writers, nothing was more basic than the fact that Abraham, Isaac, and Jacob were real people.[70] In allegory, the ideas and symbolism associated with figures are more important than the personages' actual existence. For Shires, too, it seems clear that there are only rare cases of allegorical treatment of the Bible in the New Testament. Allegory was just not a natural part of New Testament thought.[71]

Hanson's theory of Christ's presence in the Bible virtually eliminates the possibility of much allegory. Hanson postulates that there are four levels on which the Bible could have been interpreted by New Testament writers, each level one degree further removed from history: (1) real presence of Christ in Biblical history, (2) prophecy, (3) typology, (4) allegory.[72] Hanson attributes much of the New Testament's use of Scripture to the first category; the fourth category, accordingly, is not prominent.

Typology can be considered as another form of New Testament usage of the Bible. Typology, broadly defined, is "the name given to the relationships that exist between the Old and New Testaments."[73] In support of this definition, A. J. Tos cites J. Daniélou, as follows: "That the realities of the Old Testament are figures of those of the New is one of the principles of biblical theology. This science of the similitudes between the two Testaments is called typology."[74]

Daniélou understands the "science" of typology as showing

13

"how past events are a figure of events to come."[75] Daniélou explains that typology does not involve the recurrence of the same event, but rather the creation of a new event which had been "foreshadowed" by the earlier one. Gundry says, "'typological' involves reiterative recapitulation; i.e., what happens to the type happens to the antitype."[76] Shires clarifies the matter further: "The most common form of the Christian interpretation of the O.T. is typology, a kind of comparison in which the older events are seen as helping to explain and make understandable the later events but not in any way to control them."[77]

The significance of the older events, those of the Jewish Bible, is derived from what these events point to, not from the events themselves. The writers of the New Testament did not want to return to the situation of the past events: "The past is only recalled as a foundation for future hope."[78] The New Testament writers would point, for example, to the Exodus not to glorify it but to give rise to the concept of the Future Redemption. The fact that the past events (types) occurred is not as important as the new creations (antitypes) which are depicted in the New Testament.

The Rabbis employ a similar technique in the Passover Haggadah which instructs all Jews in every generation to regard themselves as if they were taken out of Egypt. This device is to create an appreciation for the concept of freedom, a value which should be sought for anew in every age. The Biblical Exodus is certainly important, but even more significant is the present and future redemption.

It is interesting to note that the prophetic books of the Bible had utilized this form, recalling the Exodus when pointing ahead to the time of Messianic redemption. The prophets made a parallel between the first deliverer and the last deliverer. Both Ellis[79] and Daniélou[80] have suggested that it was the prophetic influence that led to this use of typology in the New Testament.

Ellis, in comparing typology with allegory, claims that, while allegory concerns itself with drawing out useful and hidden ideas from a carefully assembled group of facts, typology consists in the comparison of facts themselves. So important to these facts, for the New Testament writers, is Divine intent. For the type and antitype to

14

be so closely related implies that there is a purpose worked out by a God who is responsible for both of the Testaments.[81] From the point of view of the New Testament, this Divine intent is exemplified, par excellence, in the life of Jesus.

Hanson's concern is to minimize typology, for by doing so he can show that it was Christ himself and not a type of Christ who appeared in an "Old Testament" event. "If we use the word 'typology', we are importing misleading suggestions, such as the idea that Christ was less really present in OT situations than in his incarnate life, or even that certain incidents in OT history took place primarily in order to point forward to NT times - both of which are quite absent from Paul's thought, though not from the thought of the Fathers."[82]

Nevertheless, typology remains one of the most common forms used by New Testament writers. This will hopefully become clear in our examination of the Tanakhic characters used by New Testament writers. Shires is convincing when he writes, "Christians have made the O.T., rooted though it is in the ancient past of the Jews, their own special possession whose meaning relates directly to their particular situation. Its typological interpretation, broadly conceived, is thus required."[83]

The final form to be discussed and, of course, the most relevant to this book is that of Tanakhic personages. Such personages are used both explicitly and implicitly. The explicit references will be obvious but their interpretation within this book is still required. The implicit references, those that are hidden and typological, will also be explored.

What Sources Did New Testament Writers Employ in Their Use of Scripture?

A significant hypothesis in New Testament scholarship is that of the existence of the testimony book. According to R. Harris, the testimony book was a collection of Scriptural citations intended to serve evangelists as a quick reference for missionary and polemical purposes.[84]

What considerations led to this hypothesis? First there is the reference by Melito to "six books of extracts from the Law and the

Prophets concerning the Savior and concerning all our faith. . .,"[85] plus the additional arguments advanced by Harris:

1. Recurrent quotations in the NT often agree with each other and with patristic writings in contrast to any known OT text.

2. Some of these are combined quotations suggesting a common source in which the combination already existed.

3. The same OT passages tend to be used in supporting a particular argument, and these arguments often appear under a specific concept of key-word as, for example, "stone".[86]

There have been many objections to the testimony book hypothesis. The emergence of form criticism showed that some of the alleged testimony book references were actually sayings of Jesus which could have been part of another source such as Q.[87]

The study of early Christian liturgy also poses some problems to those proponents of the testimony book hypothesis. The "center of focus was its worship and there the ordinary Christian gained and sustained his understanding of what it was all about."[88] It was in the liturgy that the real sources of anti-Jewish attitudes could be found. Harris placed a great amount of emphasis on the testimony book for the growth of anti-Jewish polemics.[89] O. Michel suggests that some of the credit that was being heaped on the testimony books should be shifted to "Paul's originality and his importance for later writers."[90] The more the latter relied on Paul, the less they used testimony books. Michel proposes that perhaps a key word (Stichwort) was used by the early Christian spokesmen and New Testament writers to suggest text combinations.[91] Therefore, there is less likelihood that an actual testimony book would have been used.

Shires does not believe that a book of testimonies even had to exist. True, there may have been some verses of the Scriptures receiving preponderant use in early Christian preaching. "Yet, the manner in which citations are employed often indicated that the Christian author had in mind not only the words but also their

16

context, which could not have been a part of a Book of Testimonies."[92] What Shires means is that a simple book of citations would not have been enough to explain the way in which they were used by the writers. On the other hand, if the book contained also the context which seems to be necessary to explain their use then the book would have been impractical and unwieldy.

After having originally subscribed to the "testimony book hypothesis", Dodd later came to reject it. Ellis summarizes Dodd's objections as follows:

1. Instances where citations of two or more NT writers agree against the LXX (Septuagint) are not numerous, "certainly not more numerous than cases where one agrees with the LXX and the other differs, or where both differ from the LXX and from one another."

2. Identical combinations of OT passages in parallel NT texts are few and perhaps special and exceptional; they are insufficient to establish general theory.

3. The recurrence of a group of passages in which "stone" stands as a symbol is striking in correspondence to a later known testimony grouping; but it is almost unique.

4. If there was a work of such importance that NT and patristic writers used it as a vade mecum, it is inexplicable that there should be no reference to it (except possibly Papias') and no extant derivative from it until Cyprian's edition in the third century.[93]

Dodd claims that the testimony book hypothesis is erroneous speculation. Dodd's major conclusion is that there was a certain oral method of Biblical study established among Christian evangelists and teachers; the testimony book resulted from that method and not vice versa.[94] In other words, the purpose of the testimony book was to compile those citations that were used predominantly in the New Testament. However, those verses were chosen by an established method of interpretation that was recognized among the Christian religious leaders. The church had a standard hermeneutical approach to Scripture.

If testimony books did exist, then surely it is possible that the way in which Biblical personages appeared in various citations would standardize their portrayal by New Testament writers. More likely, if the testimony book did not exist, then, as Dodd says, there was an established way of interpreting various Biblical passages. The same could hold true in the New Testament treatment of personages.

****

To sum up, there is convincing evidence of a strong relationship between the New Testament and Scripture. That relationship is based primarily on the search of the New Testament writers for authenticity and authority. The Bible provided the most respectable source of authenticity and the highest authority available for their audience in that historical period. There were probably several ways of appropriating Biblical material and certainly various methods of presenting that material in the New Testament. By keeping in mind these conclusions about the general relationship of the New Testament and the Bible, we can more effectively examine one of those methods of presentation, the manifestation of that relationship which is central to this book, the Tanakhic[95] personages.

Chapter I Notes

[1]Milton Steinberg, As A Driven Leaf, (New York: Behrman House, 1939), pp. 215-217.

[2]The term "Old Testament" has implications that are unacceptable to Jewish readers. From the Jewish point of view, there is only one Testament; it has not been completed, superseded, or rendered obsolete by any other. The terms Scripture(s) and Bible as used in this book will refer to the Jewish Scriptures alone, or to what Christians (in Protestant usage) call the "Old Testament".

[3]Charles Harold Dodd, The Old Testament in the New, p. 9 (hereafter cited as OT/New).

[4]Charles Harold Dodd, According to the Scriptures, p. 28 (hereafter cited as Scriptures).

[5]Henry M. Shires, Finding the Old Testament in the New, p. 15.

[6]Ibid., p. 72.

[7]Ibid., p. 22, quoting Joachim Jeremias, New Testament Theology: The Proclamation of Jesus (New York: Charles Scribner's Sons, 1971), p. 54.

[8]Ibid., p. 32, quoting A. G. Hebert, The Authority of the Old Testament (London: Faber & Faber, 1947), p. 200.

[9]Ibid., p. 34, quoting E. D. Freed, Old Testament Quotations in the Gospel of John (Leiden: E. J. Brill, 1954), p. 27.

[10]Ibid., p. 14, quoting Gerhard von Rad, Old Testament Theology, Vol. 2, translated by D. M. Stalker (new York: Harper & Row, 1965), p. 387.

[11]Ibid.

[12]Howard Clark Kee, Franklin W. Young, Karlfried Froehlich, Understanding the New Testament, p. 64.

[13]Robert Horton Gundry, The Use of the Old Testament in St. Matthew's Gospel, p. 204.

[14]Ibid., p. 199.

[15]Most scholars attribute the two animals to a case of misinterpretation. See e.g., Barnabas Lindars, New Testament Apologetic, p. 114.

[16]Infra, pp. 7ff.

[17]F. F. Bruce, <u>The New Testament Development of Old Testament Themes</u>, p.13.

[18]R. V. G. Tasker, <u>The Old Testament in the New Testament</u>, p. 53.

[19]<u>Ibid</u>., p. 53.

[20]Dodd, <u>OT/New</u>, p. 4.

[21]Gundry, <u>op</u>. <u>cit</u>., p. 3.

[22]Shires, <u>op</u>. <u>cit</u>., p. 17.

[23]<u>Ibid</u>., p. 51.

[24]<u>Ibid</u>., p. 97.

[25]E. Earle Ellis, <u>Paul's Use of the Old Testament</u>, p. 10.

[26]<u>Ibid</u>., p. 141.

[27]Shires, <u>op</u>. <u>cit</u>., p. 56.

[28]<u>Ibid</u>., p. 14.

[29]<u>Ibid</u>., p. 98.

[30]Dodd, <u>Scriptures</u>, p. 22; many scholars, however, do not regard I Peter as an early writing but rather as a pseudonymous work written around 95 C.E.

[31]Dodd, <u>OT/New</u>, p. 6.

[32]Shires, <u>op</u>. <u>cit</u>., p. 89.

[33]<u>Ibid</u>., p. 98.

[34]Ellis, <u>op</u>. <u>cit</u>., p. 137.

[35]Shires, <u>op</u>. <u>cit</u>., pp. 181f.

[36]Bruce, <u>op</u>. <u>cit</u>., p. 13.

[37]<u>Ibid</u>., quoting <u>The Documents of Vatican II</u>, English translation, edited by W. M. Abbott and J. Gallagher, (London, 1966).

[38]Dodd, <u>Scriptures</u>, p. 136ff.

[39]Anthony Tyrell Hanson, <u>Jesus Christ in the Old Testament</u>, p. 8.

[40]Ibid., p. 18.

[41]Ibid, p. 46.

[42]Ibid., p. 21.

[43]Ibid., pp. 26f.

[44]Ibid., pp. 21f.

[45]Ibid., p. 28.

[46]Ibid., p. 45.

[47]This is Hanson's interpretation of Rom. 10:20-21; ibid., p. 46.

[48]Ellis, op. cit., p. 136.

[49]Dodd, Scriptures, p. 15.

[50]Ibid., p. 12.

[51]Tasker, op. cit., p. 54.

[52]Shires, op. cit., p. 54.

[53]Dodd, Scriptures, p. 16.

[54]Antiquities, I. viii. 2.

[55]Shires, op. cit., p. 15; see also tables, pp. 183ff.

[56]Ibid., p. 122.

[57]Ellis, op. cit., p. 35.

[58]Shires, op. cit., p. 68.

[59]Ibid., p. 17.

[60]Ellis, op. cit., pp. 14f.

[61]Gundry, op. cit., p. 206.

[62]Bruce, op. cit., p. 18.

[63]"Myth & the Gospel (Contd.)," Time, March 17, 1961, p. 51.

[64]Shires, op. cit., p. 25.

[65]Ellis, op. cit., p.58.

[66]Dodd, OT/New, p. 6.

[67]Ellis, op. cit., p. 52.

[68]Ibid., pp. 53f.

[69]Supra, pp. 6f.

[70]Dodd, OT/New, pp. 7f.

[71]Shires, op. cit., p. 50.

[72]A. T. Hanson, op. cit., p. 176.

[73]Aldo J. Tos, Approaches to the Bible: The Old Testament, p. 92.

[74]Ibid., p. 93, quoting Jean Daniélou, The Bible and the Liturgy, pp. 4-5.

[75]Jean Daniélou, From Shadows to Reality, p. 12 (hereafter cited as Shadows).

[76]Gundry, op. cit., p. 209.

[77]Shires, op. cit., p. 49.

[78]Daniélou, Shadows, p. 12.

[79]Ellis, op. cit., p. 132.

[80]Daniélou, Shadows, pp. 12f.

[81]Ellis, op. cit., p. 127.

[82]A. T. Hanson, op. cit., p. 162.

[83]Shires, op. cit., p. 51.

[84]Rendel Harris, Testimonies, part 2, p. 1.

[85]Ellis, op. cit., p. 99, quoting Eusebius, Ecclesiastical History, IV, xxvi; translated by K. Lake (London, 1926) I, pp. 391f.

[86]Ibid., p. 100, quoting Harris, op. cit., part 1, pp. 8f.

[87]Ellis, op. cit., p. 102.

[88]Robert A. Spivey and D. Moody Smith, Jr., <u>Anatomy of the New Testament</u>, p. 496.

[89]Ellis, <u>op</u>. <u>cit</u>., p. 102.

[90]<u>Ibid</u>., quoting O. Michel, <u>Bibel</u>, pp. 52ff., 88ff.

[91]Ellis, <u>op</u>. <u>cit</u>., p. 102.

[92]Shires, <u>op</u>. <u>cit</u>., p. 73.

[93]Ellis, <u>op</u>. <u>cit</u>., p. 104, quoting Dodd, <u>Scriptures</u>, p. 26.

[94]Dodd, <u>Scriptures</u>, pp. 126f.

[95]The term <u>Tanakhic</u> is an adjectival form of the Hebrew word <u>Tanakh</u>, an acronym title of the Bible. It consists of the three letters T, N, Kh, each of which is an abbreviation for one section of the tripartite Scriptures: Torah (the five books of Moses), Neviim (Prophets), and Khetubim (Writings).

CHAPTER II

The Specific Use of Tanakhic Personages in the New Testament

The New Testament begins with a genealogy that mentions not less than a score of Biblical characters in only a few lines. This immediately alerts us to the prominence of Tanakhic personages in the New Testament. There are, in fact, 400 explicit references to Tanakhic personages in the 342 pages on which the New Testament is printed in the <u>Revised Standard Version Oxford Annotated Bible</u>.[1]

On the one hand, the number 400 is an inflated figure. In many cases, the personage may be cited several times within a few verses, and the references may be to only one context in the Bible. For example, if Moses' name is mentioned ten times in one chapter, the significance of each citation is diminished. On occasion, two or three Tanakhic personages appear in the same phrase, such as "God of Abraham, Isaac, and Jacob", "Adam and Eve", "Cain and Abel", etc. In these cases, the impact of the reference is singular although the use of such a phrase counts for two or three individual references in the total of 400.

On the other hand, the number 400 could also be construed as an underestimate. In Revelation and elsewhere, for example, the names of Jacob's twelve sons, Benjamin, Judah, Levi, etc., are cited only in the context of the <u>tribes</u> derived from them. Thus, their significance as personages in and of themselves is really nonexistent and therefore they were not included among the 400 and are not part of this study. Similarly, the phrase "the land of Judah" does not count as a reference to a Tanakhic personage. There are also a number of New Testament names such as Joseph and Zechariah (the fathers of Jesus and John the Baptist), which are also the names of Tanakhic personages. Generally these names are not intended to be Biblical references. Only where there seems to be an implied connection are they included in our discussion.

Most of the names in the Matthean and Lukan genealogies are also excluded as explicit references to Tanakhic personages. Many of these names are <u>hapax legomena</u> and have no outright significance other than as links necessary to bridge the more important names, such as Abraham and David (both of whom appear frequently throughout the New Testament and are thus included in our study).

27

The prophets, Isaiah, Jeremiah, Ezekiel, and Amos, to whom the New Testament frequently refers, are not counted as Tanakhic personage references. They are used only as sources for quotations and they have no role as personalities analogous to the role of other figures included in this study. It is interesting to note that although the New Testament depicts Jesus quoting these prophets very often, their role as personages is much less important that that of the earlier prophets such as Moses, Samuel, Elijah, Elisha, etc.

The number 400 also belies the importance of Tanakhic personages for New Testament writers in that many of the references, although appearing only once in an entire pericope or chapter, trigger an extended chain of thought pointing to a large context in the Bible. This phenomenon reminds us of Dodd's contention that quotations often signal the importance of a larger Biblical context.[2]

It is impossible to calculate the implicit references to Tanakhic personages; at any rate, they only emphasize further the importance of the role of Tanakhic personages in the New Testament. Many of the implicit references are treated in the third chapter of this book, even though they are not included in the following table. In the main, however, this book will limit itself to a discussion of the explicit references to Tanakhic personages.

TABLE I

Explicit References to Tanakhic Personages in the New Testament: Their Order of Appearance

Matthew: 65 References

1:1	David	9:27	David	20:30	David
	Abraham	11:14	Elijah	20:31	David
1:2	Abraham	12:3	David	21:9	David
	Isaac (2x)	12:23	David	21:15	David
	Jacob (2x)	12:39	Jonah	22:24	Moses
	Judah	12:40	Jonah	22:32	Abraham
1:3	Judah	12:41	Jonah (2x)		Isaac
1:5	Rahab	12:42	Solomon		Jacob
1:6	David (2x)	15:22	David	22:42	David
	Solomon	16:4	Jonah	22:43	David
1:7	Solomon	16:14	Elijah	22:45	David
1:17	Abraham	17:3	Moses	23:2	Moses
	David (2x)		Elijah	23:35	Abel
1:20	David	17:4	Moses		Zechariah
3:9	Abraham (2x)		Elijah	24:37	Noah
6:29	Solomon	17:10	Elijah	24:38	Noah
8:4	Moses	17:11	Elijah	27:47	Elijah
8:11	Abraham	17:12	Elijah	27:49	Elijah
	Isaac	19:7	Moses		
	Jacob	19:8	Moses		

Mark: 27 References

1:44	Moses	9:11	Elijah	12:26	Moses
2:25	David	9:12	Elijah		Abraham
6:15	Elijah	9:13	Elijah		Isaac
7:10	Moses	10:3	Moses		Jacob
8:28	Elijah	10:4	Moses	12:35	David
9:4	Elijah	10:47	David	12:36	David
	Moses	10:48	David	12:37	David
9:5	Moses	11:10	David	15:35	Elijah
	Elijah	12:19	Moses	15:36	Elijah

Luke: 73 References

1:5	Aaron	4:27	Naaman	16:25	Abraham
1:17	Elijah	5:14	Moses	16:29	Abraham
1:27	David	6:3	David		Moses
1:31	David	9:8	Elijah	16:30	Abraham
1:33	Jacob	9:19	Elijah	16:31	Moses
1:55	Abraham	9:30	Moses	17:26	Noah
1:69	David		Elijah	17:27	Noah
1:73	Abraham	9:33	Moses	17:28	Lot
2:4	David (2x)		Elijah	17:29	Lot
2:11	David	11:29	Jonah	17:32	Lot
2:22	Moses	11:30	Jonah	18:38	David
3:8	Abraham (2x)	11:31	Solomon (2x)	18:39	David
3:31	David	11:32	Jonah (2x)	19:9	Abraham
3:33	Judah	11:51	Abel	20:28	Moses
3:34	Jacob		Zechariah	20:37	Moses
	Isaac	12:27	Solomon		Abraham
	Abraham	13:16	Abraham		Isaac
3:36	Noah	13:28	Abraham		Jacob
3:37	Enoch		Isaac	20:41	David
3:38	Adam		Jacob	20:42	David
4:25	Elijah	16:22	Abraham	20:44	David
4:26	Elijah	16:23	Abraham	24:27	Moses
4:27	Elisha	16:24	Abraham	24:44	Moses

John: 32 References

1:17	Moses	6:32	Moses	8:52	Abraham
1:21	Elijah	7:19	Moses	8:53	Abraham
1:25	Elijah	7:22	Moses (2x)	8:56	Abraham
1:45	Moses	7:23	Moses	8:57	Abraham
3:14	Moses	7:42	David (2x)	8:58	Abraham
4:5	Jacob	8:5	Moses	9:28	Moses
	Joseph	8:33	Abraham	9:29	Moses
4:12	Jacob	8:37	Abraham	10:23	Solomon
5:45	Moses	8:39	Abraham (3x)		
5:46	Moses	8:40	Abraham		

Acts: 66 References

1:16	David	7:12	Jacob	7:40	Moses
2:25	David	7:13	Joseph (2x)	7:44	Moses
2:29	David		Pharaoh	7:45	Joshua
2:34	David	7:14	Joseph		David
3:11	Solomon		Jacob	7:46	Jacob
3:13	Abraham	7:15	Jacob	7:47	Solomon
	Isaac	7:16	Abraham	13:20	Samuel
	Jacob	7:17	Abraham	13:21	Saul
3:22	Moses	7:18	Joseph	13:22	David(2x)
3:24	Samuel	7:20	Moses	13:26	Abraham
3:25	Abraham	7:21	Pharaoh	13:34	David
4:25	David	7:22	Moses	13:36	David
5:12	Solomon	7:29	Moses	13:39	Moses
6:11	Moses	7:31	Moses	15:1	Moses
6:14	Moses	7:32	Abraham	15:5	Moses
7:2	Abraham		Isaac	15:16	David
7:8	Abraham		Jacob	15:21	Moses
	Isaac (2x)		Moses	21:21	Moses
	Jacob (2x)	7:35	Moses	26:22	Moses
7:9	Joseph	7:37	Moses	28:23	Moses
7:10	Pharaoh	7:40	Aaron		

Romans: 28 References

1:3	David	5:14	Adam (2x)	9:15	Moses
4:1	Abraham		Moses	9:17	Pharaoh
4:2	Abraham	9:7	Abraham	10:5	Moses
4:3	Abraham		Isaac	10:19	Moses
4:6	David	9:9	Sarah	11:1	Abraham
4:9	Abraham	9:10	Rebecca	11:2	Elijah
4:12	Abraham		Isaac	11:9	David
4:13	Abraham	9:13	Jacob	11:26	Jacob
4:16	Abraham		Esau		
4:19	Sarah				

I Corinthians: 5 References

9:9	Moses	15:22	Adam
10:2	Moses	15:45	Adam (2x)

II Corinthians: 5 References

3:7	Moses	11:3	Eve
3:13	Moses	11:22	Abraham
3:15	Moses		

Galatians: 12 References

3:6	Abraham	3:14	Abraham	4:22	Abraham
3:7	Abraham	3:16	Abraham	4:24	Hagar
3:8	Abraham	3:18	Abraham	4:25	Hagar
3:9	Abraham	3:29	Abraham	4:28	Isaac

Ephesians: No References   Phillipians: No References

Colossians: No References

I Thessalonians: No References   II Thessalonians: No References

I Timothy: 3 References   II Timothy: 2 References

2:13	Adam		2:8	David
	Eve		3:8	Moses
2:14	Adam			

Titus: No References   Philemon: No References

James: 5 References   I Peter: 3 References

2:21	Abraham		3:6	Sarah
	Isaac			Abraham
2:23	Abraham		3:20	Noah
2:25	Rahab			
5:17	Elijah			

II Peter: 2 References

2:5	Noah
2:7	Lot

2:16	Abraham	7:9	Abraham	11:17	Isaac
3:2	Moses	7:10	Melchizedek	11:18	Isaac
3:3	Moses	7:11	Melchizedek	11:20	Isaac
3:5	Moses		Aaron		Jacob
3:16	Moses	7:14	Judah		Esau
4:7	David		Moses	11:21	Jacob
4:8	Joshua	7:15	Melchizedek		Joseph
5:4	Aaron	7:17	Melchizedek	11:22	Joseph
5:6	Melchizedek	8:5	Moses	11:23	Moses
5:10	Melchizedek	9:4	Aaron	11:24	Moses
6:13	Abraham	9:19	Moses		Pharaoh
6:15	Abraham	10:28	Moses	11:31	Rahab
6:20	Melchizedek	11:4	Abel	11:32	Gideon
7:1	Melchizedek		Cain		Barak
	Abraham	11:5	Enoch		Samson
7:2	Abraham	11:7	Noah		Jephthah
7:4	Abraham	11:8	Abraham		David
7:5	Levi	11:9	Isaac		Samuel
	Abraham		Jacob	12:16	Esau
7:6	Abraham	11:11	Sarah	12:21	Moses
7:9	Levi	11:17	Abraham	12:24	Abel

I John: 1 Reference
3:12 Cain

II John: No References

III John: No References

Jude: 4 References
1:9 Moses
1:11 Cain
1:14 Enoch
     Adam

Revelation: 4 References
3:7 David
5:5 David
15:3 Moses
22:16 David

33

The table reveals many interesting facts and trends. The usage of Tanakhic personages is maintained throughout the New Testament, in eighteen of the twenty-seven books. Four of those books which do not include any explicit reference could be considered minor on the basis of their length.

There is, at the same time, a concentration of Tanakhic personages in certain sections such as Mt. 1 and Lk. 3. Even were we to remove those personages mentioned only once in the genealogies, there would still remain over twenty citations of other Tanakhic personages there. Acts 7 contains a disproportionate number of Tanakhic personages because of Stephen's speech which, in recounting Israelite history, quite naturally makes reference to these personages. Heb. 11 is known as the "roll-call" of the faithful heroes of the Scriptures wherein many of the Tanakhic personages are cited as exemplars of faith.

Except for these few areas of concentration, the Tanakhic personages are rather evenly distributed. As is expected, 263 of the 400 references appear in the Gospels and Acts, for these books form the bulk of the New Testament. If one adds Hebrews, 326 of the 400 references can be found in these six works.

The table reveals that Hebrews has the highest concentration of Tanakhic personage citations. Hebrews, encompassed within fourteen pages of the R .S. V. Oxford Bible, has sixty-three references to Tanakhic personages. I Corinthians, by contrast, which also spans fourteen pages, has only five references. On the other hand, Matthew, which has a similar number of references, sixty-five, covers forty-two pages. As D. M. Smith has pointed out, "perhaps more than any other figure, the unknown author of Hebrews deserves the title of the Old Testament theologian of the New."[3]

The writer of Hebrews shows how the Tanakhic personages fit into Christianity, comparing Abraham to Melchizedek and Jesus, showing the patriarch's inferiority; contrasting the enduring priesthood of Melchizedek and Jesus to the inferior temporary priesthood of the Jews, Levi and Aaron. Thus, because of his tendency, a desire to show the superiority of the figures of the New Testament and thus convince Christians to remain in the fold, the writer of Hebrews concentrates on relationships involving certain Tanakhic personages, namely, Abraham, Melchizedek, Levi, and Aaron. In addition, he cites a plethora of other personages in chapter 11, wherein he shows the readers how properly to perceive these figures. They are the embodiment of a faith which is strong enough to withstand the temptation of giving up their heritage. The writer pleads with his readers to do the same, to keep their Christian faith.

On the one hand, the writer of Hebrews chooses to discuss many Tanakhic personages while, on the other hand, it is clear that certain figures have a special meaning to him. Melchizedek, for example, is mentioned only by the writer of Hebrews. Similarly, Jonah and Zechariah are found only in Matthew and Luke.

An important factor in the New Testament writer's choice of Tanakhic personages is his tendency, as we have seen in the case of the author of Hebrews. Similarly, Luke, concerned with universalism, cited Tanakhic personages, such as Naaman and Elisha, who had universalistic implications associated with some events or aspects of their lives and were therefore quite naturally singled out by Luke. Universalistic Adam, not particularistic Abraham, is Luke's choice as the focus of his genealogy.

Matthew was concerned with the issue of law, for he struggled against an antinomianism that impeded the consolidation of church authority. Thus, Matthew was attracted to Moses, appropriating those aspects of Moses' life which illuminated his role as lawgiver. Jesus was then shown to go beyond Moses by being an even superior lawgiver.

Paul's interest in showing the value of faith over works led him to the use of Adam, a man who lived before there were commandments; and of Abraham, who proved to be righteous even before he performed the act of circumcision.

Of course, there is a general concern throughout the New Testament with showing the Christian Scripture superior to the Jewish Bible. Many times Tanakhic personages are used solely as foils for their New Testament counterparts. Whenever they are used typologically they are understood to be the mere shadows of the later

35

figures who do emerge.

Through an examination of each of these figures, we can hopefully arrive at an understanding of the overall role of Tanakhic personages in New Testament writings.

TABLE II

Order in Which Tanakhic Personages Appear in the Bible

Adam	Esau	Samson
Eve	Jacob (Israel)	Samuel
Cain	Levi	Saul
Abel	Judah	David
Enoch	Joseph	Solomon
Noah	Pharaoh	Ahithophel*
Abraham (Abram)	Moses	Elijah
Lot	Aaron	Elisha
Sarah (Sarai)	Joshua	Naaman
Melchizedek	Rahab	Jeremiah*
Hagar	Barak	Zechariah
Isaac	Gideon	Jonah
Rebecca	Jephthah	Esther*

* Although not explicitly mentioned in the N.T., their significance will be discussed in Chapter III.

TABLE III

Tanakhic Personages in the New Testament (Arranged Alphabetically): Their Frequency of Appearance[4]

Aaron: 5x
Lk. 1:5
Acts 7:40
Heb. 5:4
7:11
9:4

Abel: 4x
Mt. 23:35
Lk. 11:51
Heb. 11:4
12:24

Abraham: 75x
Mt. 1:1
1:2
1:17
3:9 (2x)
8:11
22:32
Mk. 12:26
Lk. 1:55
1:73
3:8 (2x)
3:34
13:16
13:28
16:22
16:23
16:24
16:25
16:29
16:30

Abraham (cont.)
Lk. 19:9
20:37
Jn. 8:33
8:37
8:39 (3x)
8:40
8:52
8:53
8:56
8:57
8:58
Acts 3:13
3:25
7:2
7:8
7:16
7:17
7:32
13:26
Rom. 4:1
4:2
4:3
4:9
4:12
4:13
4:16
9:7
11:1
II Cor. 11:22
Gal. 3:6
3:7
3:8

Abraham (cont.)
Gal. 3:9
3:14
3:16
3:18
3:29
4:22
2:16
6:13
6:15
7:1
7:2
7:4
7:5
7:6
7:9
11:8
11:17
Jas. 2:21
2:23
I Pet. 3:6

Adam: 9x
Lk. 3:38
Rom. 5:14 (2x)
I Cor. 15:22
15:45 (2x)
I Tim. 2:13
2:14
Jude 1:14

Barak: 1x
Heb. 11:32

Cain: 3x		David (cont.)		Elijah (cont.)	
Heb.	11:4	Lk.	20:44	Mk.	9:13
I Jn.	3:12	Jn.	7:42 (2x)		15:35
Jude	17:32	Acts	1:16		15:36
			2:25	Lk.	1:17
David: 59x			2:29		4:25
Mt.	1:1		2:34		4:26
	1:6 (2x)		4:25		9:8
	1:17 (2x)		7:45		9:19
	1:20		13:22 (2x)		9:30
	9:27		13:34		9:33
	12:3		13:36	Jn.	1:21
	12:23		15:16		1:25
	15:22	Rom.	1:3	Rom.	11:2
	20:30		4:6	Jas.	5:17
	20:31		11:9		
	21:9	II Tim.	2:8	Elisha: 1x	
	21:15	Heb.	4:7	Lk.	4:27
	22:42		11:32		
	22:43	Rev.	3:7	Enoch: 3x	
	22:45		5:5	Lk.	3:37
Mk.	2:25		22:16	Heb.	11:5
	10:47			Jud.	1:14
	10:48	Elijah: 29x			
	11:10	Mt.	11:14	Esau: 3x	
	12:35		16:14	Rom.	9:13
	12:36		17:3	Heb.	11:20
	12:37		17:4		12:16
Lk.	1:27		17:10		
	1:32		17:11	Eve: 2x	
	1:69		17:12	II Cor.	11:3
	2:4 (2x)		27:47	I Tim.	2:13
	2:11		27:49		
	3:31	Mk.	6:15	Gideon: 1x	
	6:3		8:28	Heb.	11:32
	18:38		9:4		
	18:39		9:5	Hagar: 2x	
	20:41		9:11	Gal.	4:24
	20:42		9:12		4:25

Isaac: 20x		Jacob (cont.)		Levi (cont.)	
Mt.	1:2 (2x)	Rom.	11:26	Heb.	7:9
	8:11	Heb.	11:9		
	22:32		11:20	**Lot: 4x**	
Mk.	12:26		11:21	Lk.	17:28
Lk.	3:34				17:29
	13:28	**Jephthah: 1x**			17:32
	20:37	Heb.	11:32	II Pet.	2:7
Acts	3:13				
	7:8 (2x)	**Jonah: 9x**		**Melchizedek: 8x**	
	7:32	Mt.	12:39	Heb.	5:8
Rom.	9:7		12:40		5:10
	9:10		12:41 (2x)		6:20
Gal.	4:28		16:4		7:1
Heb.	11:9	Lk.	11:29		7:10
	11:17		11:30		7:11
	11:18		11:32 (2x)		7:15
	11:20				7:17
Jas.	2:21	**Joseph: 8x**			
		Jn.	4:5	**Moses: 80x**	
Jacob: 24x		Acts	7:9	Mt.	8:4
Mt.	1:2 (2x)		7:13 (2x)		17:3
	8:11		7:14		17:4
	22:32		7:18		19:7
Mk.	12:26	Heb.	11:21		19:8
Lk.	1:33		11:22		22:24
	3:34				23:2
	13:28	**Joshua: 2x**		Mk.	1:44
	20:37	Acts	7:45		7:10
Jn.	4:5	Heb.	4:8		9:4
	4:12				9:5
Acts	3:13	**Judah: 4x**			10:3
	7:8 (2x)	Mt.	1:2		10:4
	7:12		1:3		12:19
	7:14	Lk.	3:33		12:26
	7:15	Heb.	7:14	Lk.	2:22
	7:32				5:14
	7:46	**Levi: 2x**			9:30
Rom.	9:13	Heb.	7:5		9:33

Moses (cont.)			Moses (cont.)			Pharaoh (cont.)		
Lk.	16:29		Rom.	9:15		Acts	7:13	
	16:31			10:5			7:21	
	20:28			10:19		Rom.	9:17	
	20:37		I Cor.	9:9		Heb.	11:24	
	24:27			10:2				
	24:44		II Cor.	3:7		**Rahab: 3x**		
Jn.	1:17			3:13		Mt.	1:5	
	1:45			3:15		Heb.	11:31	
	3:14		II Tim.	3:8		Jas.	2:25	
	5:45		Heb.	3:2				
	5:46			3:3		**Rebecca: 1x**		
	6:32			3:5		Rom.	9:10	
	7:19			3:16				
	7:22 (2x)			7:14		**Samson: 1x**		
	7:23			8:5		Heb.	11:32	
	8:5			9:19				
	9:28			10:28		**Samuel: 3x**		
	9:29			11:23		Acts	3:24	
Acts	3:22			11:24			13:20	
	6:11			12:21		Heb.	11:32	
	6:14		Jude	1:9				
	7:20		Rev.	15:3		**Sarah: 4x**		
	7:22					Rom.	4:19	
	7:29		**Naaman: 1x**				9:9	
	7:31		Lk.	4:27		Heb.	11:11	
	7:32					I Pet.	3:6	
	7:35		**Noah: 8x**					
	7:37		Mt.	24:37		**Saul: 1x**		
	7:40			24:38		Acts	13:21	
	7:44		Lk.	3:36				
	13:39			17:26		**Solomon: 12x**		
	15:1			17:27		Mt.	1:6	
	15:5		Heb.	11:7			1:7	
	15:21		I Pet.	3:20			6:29	
	21:21		II Pet.	2:5			12:42 (2x)	
	26:22					Lk.	11:31 (2x)	
	28:23		**Pharaoh: 5x**				12:27	
Rom.	5:14		Acts	7:10		Jn.	10:23	

Solomon (cont.)	Zechariah: 2x
Acts 3:11	Mt. 23:35
5:12	Lk. 11:51
7:47	

Chapter Three treats Tanakhic personages in order of the decreasing frequency of their appearance. An asterisk appearing next to the name of the Tanakhic personage indicates a departure from this order, the reasons for which should be readily apparent to the reader.

Chapter II Notes

[1]The Oxford Annotated Bible with the Apocrypha, Revised Standard Version, edited by Herbert G. May and Bruce M. Metzger, pp. 1171-1512 (hereafter cited as R. S. V. Oxford Bible).

[2]Supra, p. 11.

[3]D. Moody Smith, Jr., "The Use of the Old Testament in the New," The Use of the Old Testament in the New and Other Essays, p. 61.

[4]The references have been gathered from Nelson's Complete Concordance, edited by John W. Ellison.

CHAPTER III

The Role of Tanakhic Personages in the New Testament: Their Exegetical and Theological Function

Moses

"In the Sistine Chapel at Rome, the wall frescoes give the story of Moses on one side and the story of Christ on the other."[1] More than any other figure in Judaism, Moses stands out as the most well-known and the most respected. Moses is, after all, the major personage of four of the five books of the Pentateuch, and in New Testament times was considered the author of the Torah. It is quite understandable, then, that the writers of the New Testament, in their continual reference to the Jewish Bible, often mention Moses. In fact, Moses is cited by name more than any other Biblical personage and the implicit references to him are also quite commonplace.

Moses' importance to the New Testament writers lies chiefly in those aspects of his life and personality which are most susceptible to comparison with the life of Jesus. His significance, however, goes beyond that; he is a symbol in other ways as well. By examining Moses from a variety of perspectives, we can better understand his role as a Tanakhic personage in New Testament writings.

Moses as Historical Figure

Moses' unique career is familiar to all who read the Bible. The unusual circumstances surrounding his birth and his childhood immediately set him apart from other Biblical characters. Many of these events serve to create a pattern that is applied to Jesus himself by several New Testament writers, most notably Matthew.

The similarity begins with their birth stories. Just as Moses was hidden to avert the decree of a wicked ruler, Pharaoh, so Jesus (in Matthew's Gospel) is taken away to Egypt to escape Herod's murderous orders. Moses leaves Egypt and returns later to lead his people out. Thus, their destinations coincide in the land of Egypt. It is Matthew's clear intention and not history that paints Jesus in Moses' light. Historically, we would expect to find some evidence of a slaughter by Herod of the first born children. Other than Matthew's mention, there is none.[2]

H. M. Teeple points out that the entry into and departure from Egypt in the Gospel According to Matthew were determined by a desire to fulfill Hosea 11:1 ("Out of Egypt did I call my son").[3] The R. S. V. Oxford Bible associates the Hosea text with Ex. 4:22[4] which, in naming Israel as God's son, mentions that it is the people of Israel whom God has called.

Although Moses is not mentioned by Matthew in this opening narrative, his influence is strongly evident. Some other obvious points of comparison are suggested by Ellis: the calling out of the twelve sons of Israel, giving the law from the mount, the performance of ten miracles, and the provision of manna from heaven.[5] J. B. Tyson lists the teaching from a mountain and the transfiguration.[6] Gundry adds the shining with glory on a mountain and the institution of a covenant with blood.[7] Many of these items are found in more than one New Testament writing.

Matthew's use of Moses is reflected in the overall pentateuchal structure of his Gospel. Besides the introduction (1:1-2:23) and conclusion (26:2-28:20), there are five thematic divisions in Matthew: "Higher Righteousness" (3:1-7:29), "True Discipleship" (8:1-11:1), "Kingdom of Heaven" (11:2-13:52), "Forgiving Church" (13:53-19:2), and "Judgment" (19:3-26:1).[8] These divisions, of course, reflect the five books of Moses. The influence of Mosaic motifs is evidenced by deliberate contrasts as well as thematic similarities: e.g., in Jesus' sermon on the mount, there are six antitheses to Mosaic laws.[9]

Even the language of Matthew is closely reminiscent of the words used in connection with Moses. In Mt. 2:20, Joseph is instructed to return with the child Jesus for "those who sought the child's life are dead." This is comparable to Ex. 4:22 wherein God tells Moses, "All the men who were seeking your life are dead."

As a result of the transfiguration, Jesus' face is lit up (Mt. 17:2, II Cor. 3:7-16). This may be modeled on the statement in the Pentateuch that light shone from Moses' face as he descended Sinai (Ex. 35:29).

At the end of the their ministries, Jesus and Moses are presented in parallel language:[10] in Deut. 32:45, "Moses had finished speaking all these words. . ."; in Mt. 26:1, "Jesus had finished all these sayings."

The deaths of both men were surrounded with mystery. It is not known where Moses is buried, but Jewish tradition abounds with supernatural legends about his death. Although Jesus' burial place is revealed in the New Testament, the process of his death and resurrection have clear supernatural overtones. From birth to death, the story of Moses as a historical figure provided the New Testament writers with an ample amount of material to use in their own portrayals of Jesus.

Moses as Lawgiver

When the Hebrew Bible was translated into Greek, the word nomos replaced the word Torah. While the Hebrew term is many faceted in meaning, the Greek counterpart is almost exclusively legal. Since the New Testament writers were probably more dependent on Greek texts than Hebrew, their understanding of Moses is characterized mainly by his role as lawgiver, more so than is portrayed in the Hebrew Bible.[11]

Once again, it is Matthew who draws most heavily on the Moses material. "The delivery of the Sermon from a mountain is deliberately reminiscent of Moses' receiving the law on the mountain in the wilderness. According to Matthew, a new teaching comes from the mountain, a righteousness higher than that delivered by Moses."[12] In that sermon, Jesus contrasts his teaching to those of Moses on such things as adultery and murder, the Ten Commandments, the heart of Moses' Torah.[13]

Jesus' superiority toward the other interpreters of the law is clearly emphasized. Jesus consistently uses the pronoun "I" as in "But I say this." "Only a new Moses would speak with such authority."[14]

In Mt. 23:2-3, we find a powerful symbol of authority, "the seat of Moses," so powerful that it offsets the hypocrisy of the scribes and Pharisees: even though the scribes and Pharisees are hypocrites, according to Jesus, the people are to heed them solely because they "sit on Moses' seat." Is such a seat the equivalent of a juridical bench or majesterial throne that was customary in the first century synagogue? I. Renov believes that no such physical chair ever existed. He dismisses the claim of C. Roth that the "chair of Moses' was a Torah receptacle that was the origin of the "chair of Elijah" which came later in Jewish tradition. Renov claims that there is no

49

basis for this in Jewish sources, "ancient or modern."[15] He also points out the major problem of the seat of Moses being singular. How could many scribes and Pharisees sit on only one seat? Rather, the term "seat of Moses" is symbolic of the authority held by the scribes and Pharisees. That authority gives them the right to sit in special seats in the synagogue, as evidenced in Mt. 23:6: they love "the best seats in the synagogue."[16] These actual seats were not the "seats of Moses" but, by virtue of their sitting in "the seat of Moses", they were entitled to occupy these special seats of honor.[17] Similarly, the seat of government is in Washington, D.C. People who sit in the seat of government occupy special chairs in the Capitol and the White House, but none of these chairs is "the seat of government."

Another implication of the term "seat of Moses" could be "the heir of." M. Ginsburger says that sitting on the seat of Moses conveys the thought of succeeding someone.[18] The sense of the Matthean statement would then be that the scribes and Pharisees succeeded Moses as the leaders of the Jews in a legislative sense, an understanding that is certainly consistent with Matthew's regard for law.

J. Tepfer believes that the use of "the seat of Moses" is similar to the use of "according to the religion of Moses and Israel."[19] In both cases, the phrase justifies Rabbinical authority not derived from the Torah over the interpretation of laws and customs of the Jewish people. In the latter case, it is in the area of marriage and divorce; in the former case, it is in the area of the practices of the people in Jesus' time.[20] In any case, the use of "the seat of Moses" by Jesus in the text reflects a great respect for the authority of the interpreters of Mosaic law even if they give interpretations of which Jesus does not entirely approve.

In other instances, Jesus challenges the scribes and Pharisees vociferously. While it is true that individuals among the scribes and Pharisees in Jesus' day often opposed each other, Matthew's Jesus "exceeded the bounds of piety. . . [contrasting] his understanding of the Law to that of Moses, even though no ordinary rabbi would dare assume that kind of authority."[21]

In John's prologue, Moses and Jesus are indeed set against each other. Moses represents law, while Jesus symbolizes grace and truth.

W. A. Meeks contends that law, grace, and truth are all gifts from God, but, whereas Moses' gift is only of a superficial temporary nature, Jesus' gifts guarantee eternal life.[22]

Whereas the law has been considered a great advance in civilization, C. K. Barrett insists that Moses, at first sight, appears not to mark an advance but a set-back via commandments.[23] In Gal. 3, this is clearly stated, for the law is really of a temporary nature, like a custodian's rights over a growing child, given only as a controlling device. When the Pharisees claim that Moses, the lawgiver, told them divorce was permissible (Mk. 10:3-5, Mt. 19:7-8), Jesus explains that it was allowed only due to the hardness of the Jews' hearts. In other words, its superficial temporary nature is emphasized.

A. T. Hanson believes that, by breaking the tablets upon seeing the golden calf, Moses broke the true spiritual covenant. This was the covenant which Jesus eventually brought. The second set of tablets, the legal covenant, was given by God because of the hardness of the Israelites' hearts.[24]

In Gal. 3:19, Paul denigrates Moses' act of giving the law by removing it yet one more step from God. Paul paints Moses as a mere go-between with angels, not God, ordaining the law. This is offensive to the Jews, for, to them, Moses was a noble personage. His role as lawgiver involved interceding, advocating, and mediating with God.[25]

This further diminution of Moses' role by Paul becomes even more significant in light of the understanding that Jesus is greater than the angels. J. H. Davies maintains that the three types of figures whom Jesus supersedes are the high priest, Moses, and the angels. Davies also points out that Hebrews 2:2 explicitly states that it was the angels who brought the law.[26] Thus, Moses was a lawgiver of an inferior quality. Jesus' revelation was superior; it superseded the old and rendered it unnecessary and even problematic, for Jesus' law did not contain the demands of the Mosaic dispensation.

It is Moses' authorship of the Torah[27] (which was a universally held opinion "among Jews and Christians in Apostolic times")[28] that led to the use of his name in the New Testament as a reference point. Often, the word Moses or phrase "law of Moses" is used merely to attribute the context to Jewish Scripture. Mk. 7:10, Lk. 16:29, I Cor. 9:9, II Cor. 3:15, and Heb. 10:28 are just a few examples of this common practice.

Even more specifically, Moses is used in conjunction with the phrase "and the prophets." In this case, "Moses" definitely refers to the Pentateuch alone. In Acts 26:22, when Paul claims he has said nothing but what the prophets and Moses have said, he could be referring to Moses, the individual, and the individual prophets; or more likely, prophets could refer to the prophetic books and Moses to the Pentateuchal books. Similarly, in Acts 28:23, Paul, in speaking to Jewish leaders in Rome, tries to convince them about Jesus both from the law of Moses and from the prophets. In other words, he used the Bible.

It is questionable as to what constituted the canon at this point in history. Just how much of the Writings were included in Scripture is not definitely known. In Lk. 24:44, we can find the phrase "Law of Moses and the prophets and the psalms." It could very well be a merism referring to the Jewish Scriptures as a whole. Since "the psalms" is the opening and largest part of the writings, it could be used in a metonymic sense for the third section of the Bible. The law of Moses would be equivalent here to the first five books of the Bible. In Acts 15:21, the statement is made that Moses is read every Sabbath. This is clearly a case of metonomy, for how could a person be read? It is obvious that Moses means the five books of Moses. The reading of the Torah was thus a regular custom in the synagogue, at least as early as the time of Luke.

The transfiguration scene provides us with another symbolic use of Moses by the New Testament writers. When Jesus is on the mountain, he is accompanied by two figures: Moses and Elijah. It has been suggested that the two figures represent the heritage of the law and the heritage of the prophets. Certainly, throughout the New Testament Moses is frequently understood in terms of his association with the Pentateuch and his role as lawgiver, presenter of these books.

Moses as Mediator-Prophet
The Hebrew word nabi literally means mouthpiece. Its usage in the Bible has given it the special meaning of "mouthpiece of God" or "prophet." As we have seen, Moses' chief role was that of lawgiver.

However, the process of obtaining that law and transmitting it suggests the general meaning and role of the prophet-mediator, that is, communicator with God.

Moses' encounters with God have an interesting effect on the writers of the New Testament. It almost seems that they want to downgrade the significance of this aspect of his life. In the Gospel According to John, Moses is mentioned eleven times by name and, as Meeks observes, most of the occasions speak of the gifts of God through Moses.[29] In a sense, then, Moses is reduced to a mere channel.

Chapter 5 of that Gospel characterizes Moses' communication to God as a way in which the Hebrews were put to shame. Jesus tells the Jews that he does not accuse them to the Father, but Moses does! Jesus subtly compares his role as "prophet" with Moses. By paralleling his mission to Moses' in vv. 45-47, he is essentially saying that they have the same job, yet the Jews have placed their hope on a man who not only fails to fulfill it, but betrays his constituency. By contrast to Jesus, Moses' communication with God is seen in a negative light.

Paul, in Rom. 9:15, describes another encounter between Moses and God. In this case, Moses is told that everything depends on God's mercy, not on the action of man. Paul is showing Moses in a very unfavorable light as a deceiver, for if Moses knew this to be true, he should not have given the Jews all of the commandments. Once again, his reputation as prophet is tarnished.

Moses' role as prophet brings him into contact with the revelation of God. For A. T. Hanson, the revelation of God was always through Christ even when it occurred during Moses' time. The Christ is eternally existent. Given this assumption, Hanson explains the presence of Moses, a purely human mediator, as the prophet who gave the Jewish revelation a lower quality. "The revelation of God in Christ at the Red Sea was inferior to the incarnation; it needed a purely human mediator."[30] Christ is still responsible for giving both covenants, but in one case it is given indirectly, in the other directly.

As a prophet, Moses would certainly have encountered God. Exactly how that happened is a question with which John is concerned. Jn. 17:6, 11-12 indicates that Jesus knew the name of God; he was entrusted with it. It is very possible that these passages are modeled after the incident in Ex. 3:13-14 where Moses learns the name of God.[31]

Jn. 1:18 and 3:13 imply that even Moses never saw God's face. Glasson suggests that these citations were intended to remind the reader of Ex. 33, where Moses is not permitted to see God's face. According to this view, John wants to make it perfectly clear that Moses does not see God (but Jesus does) in order to minimize the Jews' relation to God, for they are the ones who reject Jesus.[32] Glasson also feels that perhaps John's insistence that Moses did not see God's face was an attempt to counteract the Deut. 34:10 statement that says that God knew Moses "face to face."[33]

Hanson interprets this problem differently. Since Moses could not have seen God's face, "what Moses enjoyed was a vision of Christ,"[34] This view blends very well with the way Moses is treated in Hebrews 11:24-28, which indicates that Moses had a knowledge of the Christ even as a child. Hanson points out that Michaelis, in commenting on Hebrews 11:27b, said Moses "had been granted through the visible Christ a sight of the invisible Father."[35]

The Significance of Deuteronomy 18:15 ("The Lord your God will raise up for you a prophet like me from among you, from your brethren; him you shall heed. . .")

A. J. Reines interprets Deut. 18:15 as a built-in safety device eternally protecting the validity of the Mosaic revelation. He explains that Deut. 18:15 says there will never be another Moses, for another Sinai experience would be necessary to change the law. The people would need another set of direct public empirical evidence.[36]

Some of the writers of the New Testament see Deut. 18:15 in a different light. Gundry feels that there is a significant Moses-Jesus typology in New Testament writings and that that typology is rooted at least in part in Deut. 18:15.[37]

Teeple's understanding of Deut. 18:15 is interrelated with his major thesis that the concept of a Mosaic eschatological prophet was prevalent during Apostolic times. Teeple's definition of such a prophet is "either Moses himself returned to earth or the Prophet like

Moses."[38] Tyson also feels that one of the forms of the expected messiah would be a resurrected figure of the past. He gives us as an example a Moses based on the writings of Deut. 18:15ff.[39]

There is historical evidence that various groups did have such a figure in mind, and that that figure played an important part in their theologies and liturgical expression. Jewish Christians regarded Jesus as the prophet like Moses who had been predicted in Deut. 18:15. The two figures, according to some Jewish Christians, shared human qualities, a non-virgin birth, and were even guilty of unwitting sin. For them, Jesus was the new Moses.[40]

In Rev. 11, there is allusion to the coming of two figures who very strongly resemble Elijah and Moses. Parts of Revelation are commonly regarded among scholars as reworking of a Jewish source, and Teeple concludes that the belief in Moses' return preceded the writing of the New Testament.[41]

The Samaritans' concept of a future messiah contains a prophet like Moses. The significance of Deut. 18:15 is so great that it is included as part of their Decalogue.[42]

Teeple states that Matthew is the most persistent portrayer of Jesus as a prophet like Moses.[43] Surprisingly, Deut. 18:15 is not explicitly referred to at all in the first gospel,[44] possibly because Matthew was preoccupied with Moses' lawgiving traits. Although a lawgiver is, by his very nature, a prophet in that he speaks for God, there are other implications to being a prophet. For example, one of the major roles of the Hebrew prophets was to rebuke the people, to be enforcers of God's will. Matthew was interested in Moses almost exclusively in his lawgiving capacity. He also was interested in showing Moses' law as superseded by that of Jesus and so was probably anxious to avoid any other Mosaic significance.

Deut. 18:15 emphasizes the aspect of hearing, paying heed to the prophet who will arise, Moses says, "him you shall heed." The LXX contains the words which have an even closer connection to the concept of hearing. Those words are echoed in the transfiguration scene, as Teeple points out, [45] when God says, "Listen to him [Jesus]." Mk. 4:3, 4:9, Mt. 13:18, and Lk. 8:8 are similar in their emphasis on hearing.

Acts is much less subtle in referring to Deut. 18:15. Acts 3:22 directly quotes the LXX version in speaking about Jesus as the successor of Moses whom Moses himself predicted. Teeple suggests that the preceding verse points to the restoration of former conditions,[46] the result of which is to fulfill such a prediction as Deut. 18:15. In Stephen's speech (Acts 7), Deut. 18:15 is, again, quoted verbatim.

The Gospel According to John certainly appears to recognize Moses as the center of Jewish piety. Jn. 5:46-47 is based on the assumption that the Jews are sure about Moses' authenticity as a prophet, as in Jn. 9:28-28, when the Jews chide the blind man: "You are his disciple but we are disciples of Moses. We know that God has spoken to Moses, but as for this man, we do not know where he comes from." The question of the rejection of Jesus by the Jews becomes one of the rejection of Jesus as the prophet spoken of in Deut. 18:15.[47] If one were to read Jn. 13:34 with this in mind, it might seem that Jesus tries to answer that call as the prophet of Deut. 18:15. He charges his disciples to keep the commandments which he gives them, almost as if it paralleled the command to study and obey Moses' commandments.[48]

But generally Deut. 18:15 is not significant to John. If it were, John would have to condescend to show that Jesus was the prophet like Moses. In John's eyes, there was a great polarity between Jesus and Moses just as there was between Jesus and all other human beings. Jesus was greater than Abraham (Jn. 4:53) and Jacob (4:12), and superior as well to Moses. "There is in the Fourth Gospel a recurring juxtaposition of Jesus and Moses, in which Jesus emerges as the superior."[49]

According to A. T. Hanson, it is absurd to think that John sees Jesus as the prophet like Moses. It is not Deut. 18:15 which contains Moses' description of Jesus, but rather the passages in Exodus and Deuteronomy which describe Moses meeting with God on the mountain and in the tabernacle. Moses did not prophesy of Jesus; he witnessed to the Christ whom he saw.[50]

John's attitude toward the relationship of Moses and Jesus is similar to Paul's. According to Barrett, Paul saw no typological relationship between the two personages in which one is cast as the model for the other.[51]   Since this is the thrust of the Deut. 18:15 interpretation, it probably played no role in Paul's understanding of Moses as a Tanakhic personage in New Testament writings.

Moses' Rejection by the Jews

One of the major drawbacks to being a mediator or prophet is rejection by the people such as that suffered by Moses many times. When he came down from the mountain with the tablets in his hand, he interpreted their golden calf as a rejection of God and himself, and immediately smashed the tablets. Indeed, Moses had been the butt of their rejection and impatience throughout the wanderings in the wilderness.

In the Synoptics, we see the influence of this theme of Moses' life. Immediately following the transfiguration, there is a scene of faithlessness at the foot of the mountain. Tasker submits that this parallels the Moses rejection with regard to the golden calf.[52] In Mk. 7:10, we have another illustration of Moses being rejected through his law by his people. In chastising the Pharisees, Jesus points out that the people are not observing the word of God as Moses gave it.

Lk. 22:37 is a reference to the suffering servant figure in Is. 53. Because Jesus identifies himself with that servant and because some scholars identify the servant with Moses, there is a possible implicit identification of Jesus with Moses through their sharing the rejection associated with the suffering servant.[53] This association, however, depends on the intention of the writer of this Gospel. Did Luke know that the suffering servant was modeled on Moses? Or, if Jesus himself uttered this line, did he think of the suffering servant as a reflection of Moses?

The Gospel According to John contains at least a couple of references to Moses which illustrate rejection. John's viewpoint in 5:45-47 indicates that he assumes that the Jews are not following Mosaic law. "The Jews' claim to be the true disciples of Moses would not have been accepted by the evangelist."[54] In 7:19-23, again the Jews are accused of ignoring Moses by disregarding his law.

Acts 7 contains Stephen's speech, which concerns itself with the similar treatment given Moses and Jesus by the Jews; Teeple,[55] Glasson,[56] and Tyson[57] all agree that the speech shows a clear comparison of the rejections experienced by Moses and Jesus. Tyson sums up Stephen's attitude: "You could have heard the direct utterances of Christ which Moses heard, but you were unworthy of them. Instead of that, you were given an inferior law conveyed to you not directly by Christ, but by the mediation of the angels. Even this law you failed to keep. It is not surprising therefore that when the Christ came in the most direct way of all, in the flesh. . . you failed to recognize him and put him to death."[58]

In II Timothy, we have another expression of Moses being rejected by his people. In predicting the trouble that Timothy may encounter with men who oppose him, the author of the letter presents Moses as an example of a great leader, one who represented the truth. He, too, was opposed by Jannes and Jambres. These names come from Jewish tradition but it is clear that they are merely examples of a common occurrence in the Biblical life of Moses.[59] He was a prophet who was faced with rejection. This aspect of Moses was particularly appealing to New Testament writers, for they, as Christians, faced similar situations.

Hebrews speaks of Moses' rejection in three situations. Shires suggests that in Heb. 11:2ff, Moses chooses the role as leader solely to suffer abuse for the Christ.[60] Teeple relates Jeremias' observation that there is a point of comparison between Moses and Jesus here: they both suffered.[61] Moses chose the reproach of Christ rather than to be Pharaoh's son. Tasker explains this as a prime example of Moses' faith. It was so strong that Moses was content to bear the reproach of the very people whom he wanted to help.[62] The writer of Hebrews is cautioning his readers about the rejection that Christians, in ministering to the Jews, are also bound to experience.

In the next chapter of Hebrews, the readers are reminded of the incident at Mt. Sinai wherein the Israelites rejected God. "They could not endure the order that was given" (12:20). Moses' name is mentioned and his words "I tremble with fear" are quoted here to remind them of the rejection which he met. The writer of Hebrews is saying, "You be different."[63] At Sinai the people did not want to hear the command. "If they did not escape when they refused him who warned them on earth, much less shall we escape if we reject him who warns from heaven" (12:25).

Moses is recalled in Heb. 3:16 in a situation that shows he was unable to be an effective leader. More significant than Moses' failure, however, is the Israelites' continued rejection of their leader and their lack of faith.

Moses as Priest

One of the major themes of the Book of Hebrews is Jesus' role as priest. While this is done primarily with reference to Melchizedek, there are several occasions in which Moses appears for this purpose.

Chapter three of Hebrews stresses Jesus' superiority to Moses in terms of their relationship to "God's house." The beginning of the chapter identifies Jesus as apostle and high priest and immediately follows with the Jesus/Moses comparison. The notion of Moses as priest was possibly a widely accepted one, and was one of which the writer of Hebrews was aware; J. H. Davies believes he was influenced by Philo, who refers to Moses as high priest.[64]

Heb. 8:5 recalls Moses being addressed by God with regard to the building of the sanctuary. According to this verse, Moses had seen the heavenly sanctuary and was now to duplicate it with a copy on earth. "See that you make everything according to the pattern which was shown you on the mountain." (8:5). Davies points out that, according to Philo (Life of Moses ii, 74), Moses had seen the heavenly sanctuary.[65] One need not assume that the writer of Hebrews had to have been influenced by Philo in this case for Ex. 25:40 explicitly says that Moses was shown details of the heavenly sanctuary while on the mountain.

Heb. 8:2 contains a reference to the "true tent" in which Jesus ministers, one that is far superior to that of Moses, which was pitched far outside the camp (Ex. 33:7). By contrast, Jesus' is the "true tent" and is set up by the Lord, not man, thus emphasizing that Moses' tent was merely a copy.

Heb. 9:11-22 details the sealing of the covenant. Moses seals it only with the blood of calves and goats; Jesus seals the new covenant with his own blood. The purpose of this reference in Hebrews could very well be twofold. On the one hand, it shows that blood is an essential part of the covenant. On the other hand, it reiterates the basic theme: Jesus is greater than Moses, for in every respect, even in the use of his own blood rather than that of animals, he goes beyond what Moses did.

As Davies indicates, Heb. 9:19 contains a misinterpretation of the process of the sprinkling of the blood and recitation of the commandments. Thus, the writer was probably quoting the process from memory of the text or from an oral tradition rather than from an open text in front of him.[66]

The sealing of the covenant involves blood, and it is Jesus' crucifixion that is regarded as the seal of the new covenant. Glasson speculates that the description of blood and water flowing from Christ's side (Jn. 19:34) may have some relation to Moses in Rabbinic literature. It is interesting, although inconclusive, that in Shemot Rabbah, Moses strikes the rock twice, the first time drawing blood, the second time water.[67] The parallels are there: blood, water, Christ as the rock. The problem of dating the origin of the midrash and the question of dependency of New Testament on Rabbinic tradition or vice versa render such observations speculative.

Moses as Miracle Worker

It must be admitted that the process described in Lev. 14 for the cure of leprosy has mysterious overtones. After his miraculous curing of a man with that ailment, as described in the Synoptic Gospels, Jesus specifically refers to the process as "that of Moses" (Mk. 1:44, Mt. 8:4, Lk. 5:14).

In Matthew, this healing of the leper by Jesus is just the first of ten miracles by him: (1) healing of the leper (8:2-4); (2) healing of the centurion's servant (8:5-13); (3) eliminating the fever of the mother-in-law in Peter's house (8:14-15); (4) calming of the storm on the sea (8:23-26); (5) casting out the demons (8:28-32); (6) healing the paralytic (9:6); (7) resuscitating the ruler's daughter (9:18); (8) relieving the woman with hemorrhages (9:20-22); (9) giving sight to the blind (9:27-30); (10) giving speech to the dumb demoniac (9:32-33).

The arrangement of these miracles is deliberate. Teeple points out that just as Moses performs his ten miracles before he collects his people and starts his journey, so Jesus does before he calls his disciples and goes on his mission.[68] Teeple seeks further support in his argument by H. J. Schoeps: that the belief that Moses performed the ten wonders was prevalent in the Jewish mind of those days. Pirke Avot, which attributes many of its aphorisms to first century figures, and whose underlying traditions could date from this period, speaks of the ten wonders by the sea (5:5).[69]

R. H. Smith finds a similar typology of signs and miracles in the Fourth Gospel, guided by the underlying theme that "what was performed by key Hebrew figures in the past was imperfect and is now recapitulated by Jesus in a perfect way.[70] In the Fourth Gospel, Jesus is disgusted by the Jews' need for signs. This, says Smith, is parallel to Pharaoh's hardness of the heart. Smith builds a comparison of Moses' ten plagues to combat Pharaoh's stubbornness with the signs that Jesus gives. Each of the examples has Moses emerge as an imperfect, destructive, negative signgiver, with Jesus representing complete, constructive, beneficial acts.

Moses changed water to blood before the eyes of the Pharaoh. Jesus changed water to wine, the blood of the grape, a life-giving substance. Moses brought a plague on domestic animals. The two important characteristics of this act for John are that it was an affliction that led to death, and that it resulted indirectly in the Pharaoh's suffering. The parallelism (Jn. 4:46f.) lies in the fact that this, too, was an affliction that would have led to death. It involved indirect suffering to the subject, the official. It was his son who would have died thus causing suffering to the official himself. Smith admits that the parallelism of this sign is weak.[71]

The next sign of Moses is the affliction of Egyptians with sores. This is the first real, direct, personal, bodily affliction as is the lameness of the man who is healed by Jesus (Jn. 5:2-9). Once again Moses brings debilitation while Jesus restores to health. Moses summons thunderstorms to bring devastating hail, while Jesus stills the storm (Jn. 6:16-21). Moses brings locusts which eat the food and fruit of the land, consuming its sustenance; Jesus feeds the multitude with bread. Moses causes darkness to reign over the land resulting in a total blindness of the people; Jesus brings sight to a blind man. Finally, death comes to the firstborn of the Egyptians; the New Testament offers the story of the raising of Lazarus, bringing someone back to life, and it also tells of Jesus' resurrection from death. Jesus, incidentally, was a firstborn.

These, then, are the seven parallel signs of Moses and Jesus. Smith claims that there are seven rather than ten due to a first century tradition in which these plagues number only seven. John removed the second, third, and fourth plagues to arrive at this number. Smith describes these plagues as "colorless".[72]

Another of Moses' signs is seen in Num. 21:8-9 when he lifts up the brazen serpent. To the uninformed reader of the Jewish Bible, it would appear that Moses is making wonders, doing magic by creating this simple healing device for all who are snake-bitten. Jn. 3:14-15 makes use of this incident as allegedly foreshadowing Jesus' death on the cross. Hanson,[73] Meeks,[74] and D. M. Smith[75] all agree that the lifting up of the serpent in the wilderness is a type for Christ being lifted up on the cross. Just as the lifting of the serpent saved the Israelites who were dying from snake-bite so Jesus being lifted up in the cross saved all from their sins.[76] The snake gave the people extended life; Jesus gives eternal life. This kind of typology is labeled terminal typology for it is limited and not necessary to a larger scheme. As Smith points out, in this instance, Jesus is compared to the serpent, while later, Jesus is typed after Moses as a miracle worker.[77] Justin Martyr insisted that it was not a mere brazen serpent that Moses lifted up, but rather a cross which protected the people from snakes.[78]

The story of the giving of the manna to the Israelites in the wilderness (Ex. 16) is cited by John in 6:32. In the exodus account, Moses' role as mediator of this miraculous gift is described in a positive sense; he is the miracle worker, explaining the secrets of how to survive in the wilderness with this mysterious substance. John, however, denigrates the role of mediator, minimizes its significance, and focuses instead on God, the Father, as the source of the gift. Moses, once again, is cast in a negative light, especially when compared to Jesus' role. "Christ does what Moses could never do; he gives the 'true bread from Heaven,' which afford eternal life to the world.[79] Jn. 6:49 points out that those who ate the manna eventually died. The manna, therefore, did not really "sustain" them. Jesus' gift, symbolized by the multiplication of the loaves, is the real bread which gives eternal life.[80] For Paul, the Eucharist is the symbol of the true sustenance.

In addition, A. T. Hanson claims that the real giver of the manna was Christ himself.[81] The Exodus text reads: "This is the bread which Kyrios has given you to eat." Hanson believes that whenever the word Kyrios appears as one of God's names, it indicates Christ.

Another possible reference to Moses as a miracle worker, a doer of signs, is appropriately in the mysterious book of Revelation. Rev. 11:3-13 describes the story of God's two witnesses. One of them is said to have the power to change water into blood and cause plagues, apparently an implicit reference to Moses.

Moses as Deliverer

The first book in Scripture where Moses appears derives its name from its theme: the Exodus from Egypt, deliverance from bondage to redemption. The association of Moses with the role of deliverer is one, therefore, that is hard to overlook. The redemption to which Moses led the children of Israel served as a type for which to strive as early as the days of the Hebrew prophets, after the first Exile. The deliverance is an idealized one, symbolizing political freedom for the oppressed. It led to a messianism, a hope that God would one day bring the end of days, a time when oppression and tyranny would cease. Accordingly, Teeple believes that, after the exile, Moses was made a great hero. It is only a small step to identify him with the figure of the prophet-king-messiah who would usher in this idyllic time.[82] Glasson maintains that "there can be little doubt that this particular form of messianic hope originated in the pre-Christian period."[83]

Meeks points out that there was a tension between the influence of a Davidic Messiah tradition and a Mosaic tradition. The Mosaic figure prevailed as it combined eschatological, royal, and prophetic qualities.[84] Moses, indeed, became the dominant figure in the Jewish religion. Specifically, he became "the central figure in the drama of redemption."[85] Teeple agrees, describing Moses as hero par excellence, founder of the nation, superior to all other prophets, and a model for future leaders.[86] However, there is also a tendency to limit him, perhaps because so much had been done to glorify him. Moses is not the prophet, but only one of many.[87]

In order to prevent Moses from becoming an idol, a superhuman personage, Rabbinic literature stresses that God was the executor of the Mosaic deliverance, and that Moses was only an instrument. Moses is not even mentioned in the Passover Haggadah;

God is the dominant figure.

The fact that the Exodus served as a prototype of the Messianic redemption gives us strong reason why Moses was singled out as a precursor of Jesus. Other personages of the first century had claimed to be messianic. Jeremias believed that conditions of the first century led people to hope that a Mosaic type deliverer would arise to defeat Rome.[88] In Josephus (Antiquities XX:v:l), Theudas gathers together a following and leads them to the wilderness in preparation for redemption from the wicked king, and even claims to divide the sea for them.

One must be careful about placing too much emphasis on Moses/Jesus typology for Jesus is really the new Israel, not the new Moses.[89] In Ex. 4:22, it says "Israel is my first-born son," indicating that the people were regarded as the son of God. Jesus' identification as God's son matches him with the people of Israel, not with Moses. Even Matthew, who more closely than any other New Testament writer suggests that Jesus resembled Moses, if only as a lawgiver, recognized a basic difference: that Jesus was to be worshipped. "In Judaism, Moses never occupied the exalted position of Jesus. . ."[90] Teeple does not admit that the early Christian writers accepted the Mosaic prophet-king role for Jesus. Jesus had failed to deliver Israel out of Rome's control. The mere fact that he was arrested and killed negates that politically oriented role. Teeple suggests that the association of Jesus with such a role would interfere with the writers' efforts to placate Rome's attitude toward the Christians.[91]

Still, the comparison of Jesus and Moses as savior looms large. "As Moses leads an oppressed people out of Egypt, so Jesus might free a world oppressed by the burden of sin."[92] The early Christian liturgy contains many prayers with a distinct parallel of Moses-Exodus-Jews to Jesus-Salvation-Christians.[93] Tasker believes that Jesus' role as redeemer of Israel was so important that, in his baptism, he received a divine revelation, similar to that of Moses when he was summoned. That revelation made them conscious of their roles as redeemers.[94]

Perhaps the role of redeemer should be understood more in its eschatological orientation, a point of view that is evident in the Fourth Gospel. Just as Matthew found Moses' role as lawgiver vital, John finds the early redemption in the salvation history of Israel the type for Jesus' role.[95]

The writer of Hebrews, searching the Bible for examples of faith, finds an excellent additional illustration in this aspect of Moses. Heb. 3:7-19 tells us that Moses was the leader who led the Israelites out of Egypt to a new land. Jesus also leads to a new land: heaven! It was lack of faith that kept the Israelites from entering; therefore, Christians must be faithful.[96]

The wandering through the wilderness was an integral part of the process of salvation. In Matthew there is a strong comparison of Jesus' temptation in the wilderness with that of the Israelites.[97] Interestingly enough, Mt. 4, describing the victories of Jesus over the devil, uses quotations from Deuteronomy which deal with the Hebrews' temptations;[98] i.e., Jesus tells the devil the same type of things that Moses tells the Hebrews.

It should be pointed out that the duration of the temptation in the wilderness was forty days and nights. While that coincides with the duration of the flood, it is also the length of time that Moses spent on Mt. Sinai and the number of days Elijah spent on his sojourn. For Moses those forty days served as the time in anticipation of the founding of Israel as a people. For Jesus, that was the time spent in anticipation of the founding of the new Israel.[99]

Paul's letter to the Corinthians also draws upon the theme of salvation and therefore alludes to Moses as deliverer. In order to achieve salvation, the Israelites had to wander through the wilderness. I Cor. 10:1-4 uses the wilderness wanderings as a type for the Christian life:[100] the Christian, too, must "wander through the wilderness" before salvation can occur.

Moses as King - Enthroned One
The preceding section on salvation covered Moses' messianic-prophetic-royal mission. Moses can also be seen as the purely royal enthroned figure who is so important to John's Gospel and the Synoptics in the transfiguration of Jesus.

One of the central themes in the Gospel of John is the ascension of Jesus, his enthronement as king of Israel. One might point to an implicit parallel with Moses who, according to some strata of Rabbinic and post-Biblical literature, did not die but "was translated, ascended, and serves on high."[101] However, a striking inconsistency in this suggestion is the fact that Jesus' glorification in the Fourth Gospel takes place through his death on the cross, while Moses' royalty derives from the Sinai theophany where he was "enthroned in heaven."[102] It was at that point and not at his death that Jesus' ascent, leadership, and role as intercessor came to light. Meeks suggests that there is evidence that Jesus' enthronement could parallel Mandean gnostic myths and therefore have little to do with Moses traditions.[103]

For the Synoptics, the transfiguration is the scene of Jesus' glory. There are several parallels between it and the Sinai theophany. Moses' presence (along with Elijah) at the transfiguration suggests a relationship between the two events. Tasker proposes that Moses and Elijah represent the two most important parts of the Bible: Law and Prophets, and their presence is an indication of Jesus' close relationship to them, for Jesus, in his study of Scripture, becomes engulfed in their lives so much that he becomes like them.[104] He resembles Moses as a redeemer. Teeple explains that there are other reasons for their appearance: to give authority as Messianic witnesses, to show that Christ replaces Moses and Elijah as authority, and to connect Jesus with the Jewish hope that Moses and Elijah would come together to usher in the kingdom of God.[105] This association of Moses and Elijah is possibly an early Rabbinic tradition which has been traced to a quote by Johanan b. Zakkai in Deuteronomy Rabbah.[106]

The transfiguration and the death on the cross serve as points of glorification of Jesus which parallel Moses being made royal on Mount Sinai. R. F. Johnson claims that the placement of the transfiguration between the first two predictions of the Passion testifies to its significance in the Gospel According to Luke.[107]

Moses as Servant of God
Num. 12, a comparison of Moses with Miriam and Aaron, refers to Moses as a servant. While God speaks to Moses' siblings in dreams and visions, "not so with my servant Moses; he is entrusted with all my house." Even as a servant, Moses is superior to his siblings, for God speaks to him "face to face."

The writer of Hebrews also calls Moses the servant of God and by contrast calls Jesus the Son of God. No matter how close God is to Moses as a servant, Jesus has a closer relationship, for he is the son in God's household (Heb. 3:2); they may both be faithful, but one has family rights.

The use of different prepositions magnifies the contrast. As servant, Moses is in the household, passing directions on from the "owner" to the other servants. Jesus is over the house, having the authority to dictate the commands himself.[108]

A. T. Hanson sees something even deeper than the servant/son comparison in Heb. 3:3. Num. 12 itself defined the Moses/Christ relationship. The word Kyrios, a signal that Christ is meant, is employed in Num. 12 indicating that Moses was then seen as Christ's servant. When Hebrews speaks of God's house, it thus means Christ's house. Naturally, Christ is worthy of more honor than Moses, his servant. Christ is seen ultimately as the builder (owner) of the house.[109]

Moses as Collective Symbol of the Jewish People
Because of Moses' leadership, in Heb. 3 he is used metonymically as a collective symbol of the Jewish people. That leadership, however, according to Hebrews, failed to live up to God's expectations.

The most obvious example of Moses in this role occurs in I Cor. 10:2, which says that "all [the Israelites] were baptized into Moses." Certainly, the expression "baptized into Christ" is a common one but "into Moses" is found only here. It seems fairly obvious that this was based on the Christian formula and that Paul was responsible for the introduction of the phrase. Barrett explains that the Israelites were incorporated into Moses. The use of the phrase "into Moses" is a good example of how Moses is understood in the light of Christ and not vice versa. It supports the contention that, for Paul, Jesus is not a new Moses.[110]

Moses' Relationship to Joshua
Moses' relationship to Joshua parallels Jesus' relationship to his disciples. Glasson presents four items of evidence from the Gospel According to John: (1) In Midrash Rabbah, Moses hands over his

authority to Joshua and temporarily serves him. In Jn. 13:1, Jesus serves his disciples. (2) Moses, in Num. 27:20, gives his glory to Joshua; Jesus does the same to his disciples in Jn. 17:22. (3) Moses ordains Joshua in Deut. 36:9; Jesus does the same in Jn. 20:22 and 15:16. (4) Joshua is called to be a shepherd in Num. 27:17; Peter, one of the disciples, is summoned to do the same in Jn. 21:15-17, 10.[111] Jesus' relationship to his disciples apparently draws upon another Mosaic similarity: in Ex. 18:13ff., Moses appoints seventy elders; in Lk. 10, Jesus appoints seventy disciples.[112]

Moses as Shepherd

The major character of the Scriptures who is known as the shepherd is, of course, David the King. However, there are also places where Moses is identified as a shepherd. Ex. 3:1 pictures Moses tending the flock of his father-in-law, Jethro, when God calls him in the wilderness. Meeks hypothesizes that "Moses' designation as a shepherd is closely connected with both his prophetic and royal functions.[113]

Jn. 10 speaks of the concept of "hearing the voice of the shepherd." Meeks suggests that this alludes to hearing God's voice through Moses' words at the theophany at Sinai.[114]

J. H. Davies suggests another implicit reference to Moses as the shepherd in Heb. 13:20 when Jesus is called the great shepherd of the sheep.[115] Since Jesus has taken Moses' place, he must fill the latter's role as shepherd.

Moses as Teacher

When Moses is recalled by Jews today, it is most often as the first part of the hyphenated Moshe-Rabbenu, meaning Moses, our teacher. B. J. Zlotowitz feels that throughout the ages, Jews have emphasized that title rather than Servant of God, since Christians used "servant" so predominantly to refer to Christ.[116]

It is the role of teacher that Moses occupied which lends itself as a model for the missionaries in their instruction of Christian believers. In I Cor. 10, Paul is instructing Christians and uses Moses with the Israelites as an example of a leader teaching his followers.[117] Barrett sees Moses as a paradigm of the Christian minister, such as Paul, rather than as a type for Christ.[118]

A. T. Hanson maintains that the differences between Christian ministers, such as Paul, and Moses is greater than their apparent similarity. Moses, in teaching, had veiled the truth of Christ, while Paul reveals.[119]

The Veil of Moses

In Ex. 34:29-35, Moses veils his face after coming down from the mountain. Apparently, his face was shining so brightly as a result of his talking with God that it was extremely uncomfortable for anyone to look at him. II Cor. 3 refers to this passage, explaining that the brightness on Moses' face would eventually fade because of the temporary nature of his dispensation.[120] Paul turns that veil into a meaningful symbol. J. W. Doeve claims that Paul is using the same hermeneutics in dealing with the veil as did the Rabbis in the synagogue.[121] In other words, he is making a Christian midrash. The Israelites in Paul's time were like Moses in that they had veils over their minds preventing them from seeing the real light of Jesus Christ. Tasker defines the veil as a symbol of the imperfection of the Jews' understanding of Scripture.[122]

In vs. 16 of this chapter, the phrase "turn to the Lord" indicated the way in which a person can remove the veil. That same phrase in the Jewish Bible means turning to the law of Moses. To Paul, however, it means for a Jew to convert to Christ.[123]

For A. T. Hanson, a typology of Moses and Christ does not exist here. Rather, the point of comparison is Moses and Paul. They were both given the same mission: to reveal Christ to the world. Moses wore the veil as a means of preventing the revelation of Christ from spreading to others. If the Jews saw the brightness of Moses' face, they would be aware that he had seen Christ and then they would know that the law was only temporary. Their obligation to observe it would become void after Christ's incarnation.[124] By wearing the veil, Moses was protecting the eternity of his own dispensation. By contrast, Paul, faced with the same task, chooses to reflect Christ.[125]

The veil also serves as a symbol of nonbelief, and the veiled Moses cited in Scripture is the model of a nonbeliever. Since Moses had hid Christ from them, the Jews were still wearing the veil themselves in Paul's day. In the New Testament any nonbeliever is one whose face is veiled; it can be removed by turning to Christ.[126]

Moses as a Man of Faith

Hebrews had a more positive outlook on Moses' faith than does Paul. Its author is willing to accept Israel's traditional heroes "as figures above criticism" because of their extraordinary faith in God. A. T. Hanson explains that the traditional understanding of Moses leaving Egypt after the murder of the taskmaster should be reevaluated, postulating that Moses does not leave out of fear of the wrath of the king, rather out of faith in God.[127] Heb. 11:27 leaves out any mention of Moses being afraid, and the only fear that Moses experiences is the fear of the wrath of God in Heb. 12:21.

J. H. Davies cites five examples of faith in conjunction with Moses in Heb. 11. The first is via his parents in that they showed faith by disobeying Pharaoh's orders about Israelite male children. Next, Moses prefers not to be called Pharaoh's son and leaves the royal household, killing the Egyptian and identifying with his people. Third, he flees to the desert in the faith that God would protect him. Fourth, he obeys God's command about the Passover, having faith that the firstborn of the Israelites would be spared. Finally, he crosses the Red Sea, confident in the faith that God would secure their passage.[128]

The fact that the early Christian community considered itself primarily as a community of faith magnifies the need for an important prototypal figure such as Moses in their writings.

Abraham

Perhaps the most popular Biblical image of Abraham is as the father of the Jewish people. In the New Testament, too, we find that this role is emphasized.

In the Synoptic Gospels, Abraham is mentioned almost exclusively in his patriarchal role. In Mt. 3:9, John the Baptist chastises the "Pharisees and Sadducees" who come for baptism. He tells them not to be so presumptuous as to think that, because they are descended from Abraham, they are exempt from bearing "fruit that befits repentance." The use of Abraham here clearly shows that a racial link is presumed. Matthew, in fact, belittles this racial link by pointing to God's ability to create even more children of Abraham merely from stones. In Matthew's view, the claim of descendancy from Abraham is not compelling.

In Lk. 19:9, Zacchaeus, the tax collector, vows to give money to the poor and to follow the laws in making restitution. The explanation is given that he is a "son of Abraham" and therefore seeks forgiveness according to the way expected of him. The focus on his relationship to Abraham merely shows that he is a Jew, a physical descendant of Abraham.

In Acts 13:26, this understanding of Abraham is continued. "Brethren, sons of the family of Abraham and those among you that fear God. . ." This is Paul's salutory greeting to a crowd of Jews and gentiles. The acknowledgment of the ancestry of the Jews is linked to Abraham, their first father.

Hebrews also uses Abraham in this manner. Heb. 2:16 speak of the descendants of Abraham in contrast to angels. The Jews are flesh-and-blood human beings, not angels. The "seed of Abraham" should be interpreted literally. Here, Abraham is once again the father of the Jewish people. Another implication of this passage is that God is "concerned" with the Jewish people who are the elected through Abraham. According to Davidson, this passage shows that "the believing Hebrews are in the view of the author the People of God."[1]

Paul does not make much use of Abraham as the physical ancestor of the Jewish people. His concentration is on Abraham as the spiritual ancestor of believers in Christ. However, when he writes to the Romans and Corinthians, Paul uses Abraham in the same sense that the Synoptic writers and the writer of Hebrews do. Apparently, his background is called into question. Responding to this, Paul claims that he is a descendant of Abraham (Rom. 11:1, II Cor. 11:22), thus, giving himself some credentials and authority with which to address them. He is, after all, part of the "chosen people."

In general, the early Christians identified themselves as sons of Abraham. "Jesus surely felt himself to be a son of Abraham. . ."[2] In chapter I of this book we explained the desire on the part of early Christians to maintain a continuity between the "old covenant" and their alleged new one.[3] Linking themselves racially with Abraham certainly is in consonance with this understanding.

That principle is expressed via the Matthean genealogy which begins with Abraham and culminates in Jesus. There are three divisional groups in the genealogy: the first, from Abraham to David; the second, from David through the Babylonian deportation; and the third, from the Babylonian deportation through Christ. Each of these groups is bracketed by significant historical events: Abraham, David, the Babylonian deportation and Christ are all vital to the Christian. Abraham's importance derives from his being the first Jew and father of the people. In Acts 7, Stephen's speech, a recollection of important historical Biblical events, begins with Abraham.

In Luke, Abraham does not bear the same significance. He no longer commences the genealogical list but, by being placed in the middle of the names, becomes only one link from Adam through Jesus. The reason for this is not that his role as father of the Jewish people is denied, but that Luke is interested in showing the universalism of Jesus and Christianity. To trace the genealogy only back as far as Abraham would, accordingly, have been inappropriate.

The idea of descent becomes extremely important to Paul, but for him, the definition of descent changes. The "crux issue" is whether descent is by body or by faith.[4] This contrast is exemplified in Gal. 3:16 when Paul constructs an argument on the basis of the word "seed" in God's promise to Abraham, emphasizing the singular nature of the word. Paul contends that the seed, if singular, can only refer to one type or set of descendants, those of faith, excluding those of body.[5] The problem with Paul's argument is that the word and concept "seed" can be plural, thus referring to all descendants of Abraham, whether by faith or body.

That the promise is directed only to one descendant and not the other is consistent with early Jewish tradition. The "seed" was always concentrated in one person: Isaac and not Ishmael, Jacob and not Esau. Paul also saw the seed of Abraham concentrated in one person: Jesus Christ.[6] The allegory in Gal. 4:22, wherein Hagar and Ishmael are contrasted with Sarah and Isaac, provides an additional illustration of Paul's attitude in this regard. The son of the promise is Isaac because he is not just the racial descendant but the spiritual

72

descendant. It was for this reason alone that the connection to Abraham belonged to him.

For Paul, the true offspring of Abraham are Christ and his followers. The Jews, by concentrating so much on the Law, have cut themselves off. They are the purely physical descendants. The Christians are the real offspring in that they show faith, which was first manifested in Abraham's own trust in God.[7] There are numerous examples of this message in Paul's writings: Rom. 4, Rom. 9:7, Gal. 3-4. The underlying principle is that Abraham is the father of all who share his faith, not just his genes. The moral and spiritual sense predominates over the physical.

John's sole usage of Abraham is found in chapter 8 of his Gospel. The Jews whom Jesus is confronting argue that they are descendants of Abraham and therefore do not need Christ, for they already have all the merit they require. Jesus points out that they are not really descendants of Abraham in that they do not have the requisite faith. In other words, the same principle that Paul used, that of spiritual descendancy, is operative here. John denigrates the physical connection and emphasizes the importance of faith.

The letter of James seems to provide an alternative view. His use of Abraham in 2:21 is followed by the description: "our father." Tasker believes the implication here is that Abraham is the father of the new Israel as well as the old.[8] In other words, James, in keeping with his more "Jewish" approach to Christianity, would argue that physical descendancy and spiritual descendancy are equally valid in claiming Abraham as ancestor.

Abraham provides the New Testament writers with numerous examples of faith. Hebrews 11 contains the "roll call" of Scriptural personages who exhibited faith during their lives. Abraham did such by leaving his father's house; by sojourning in a foreign land in tents, without a permanent residence; by believing that at the age of ninety-nine he would sire a child; and by showing his willingness to sacrifice that child, Isaac.

The sacrificing of Isaac is also construed as implying Abraham's belief in resurrection.[9] Why else would Abraham be willing to destroy the possibility of the covenant's fulfillment, unless he knew that Isaac would return to life? Ellis believes this faith in the miracle of the resurrection is the "bedrock of Pauline thought" on faith and underlies Gal. 3.[10] Barrett disagrees. He believes that the faith spoken of in Gal. 3, as well as in Rom. 4, is faith on Abraham's part with regard to having a son born.[11]

The book of Acts contains Stephen's speech recounting the history of Israel, beginning with Abraham in Mesopotamia. He also points out Abraham's acts of faith: Abraham left his father's house, he circumcised Isaac, he believed in God's promise so much that he was satisfied that it would not be fulfilled in his lifetime but in that of his posterity.

God's promises to Abraham play an important role in the New Testament. The Magnificat in Luke I ends with the father of John the Baptist acknowledging that his son's birth is part of the fulfillment of God's promise to Abraham.

The word "promise" in association with Abraham immediately brings to mind the Akedah and Abraham's relationship to Isaac, because of the essential promise made to Abraham as a result. J. H. Davies thinks that Abraham only began to have his promise fulfilled with the birth and growth of Isaac but that the writer of Hebrews 11 shows that the promise was not fulfilled until Christ.[12] The book of Acts reflects that same attitude in 3:25 when it refers to God's promise to Abraham in terms of Jesus' coming in fulfillment of Gen. 22:18: "and in your posterity shall all the families of the earth be blessed."

Abraham's faith is frequently recalled in connection with the promises made to him. Davidson says that Abraham's faith was manifest not in being called, nor in realizing it was God's voice, but in "realizing the promises accompanying the call."[13]

Abraham thus serves as a perfect type for both the Christian believer and Christ himself. Barrett says the Abraham prefigures the Christian believer in that he puts his trust in God's power to accomplish the seemingly impossible.[14] Spivey and Smith claim that underlying Rom. 4:1-25 and Gal. 3 is the understanding that Abraham's faith is the prototype for Christ on the cross. "Abraham, the father of Israel, shows that faith in God's promise has from the beginning of the story of salvation been man's proper attitude before God."[15] L. Hicks concurs in calling Abraham "a monumental figure of faith . . . a model for all Christians . . . prototypical of Christ's life of perfect obedience."[16]

Abraham's Bosom

The story of the rich man and Lazarus appears in Lk. 16:22ff. Lazarus, a righteous soul, dies and goes to Abraham's bosom, while the rich man, presumably not a good person, dies and goes to Hades where he is tormented. Part of that torment derives from his seeing Lazarus enjoying himself, finding comfort in Abraham's bosom. It is a mythical supernatural image[17] which is "practically equivalent to 'Paradise.'"[18]

It is possible that this place is so named because Abraham was a typical example of the type of person who achieved such bliss. In any case, it is such a desirable place that the rich man implores Abraham that, if he himself cannot achieve such paradise, then at least his children should be forewarned so that they might arrive there. The conversation with Abraham provides an additional supernatural touch to this already mystical experience and presumes Abraham to be somehow alive.

This same kind of image is expressed in Mt. 8:4 and Lk. 13:28 wherein Abraham, along with Isaac and Jacob, are in the kingdom of heaven, sitting at a table waiting for other righteous people to join them. In Matthew, the centurion is told that he will sit there for he has faith, the kind of which the Jews themselves are lacking. The image of Abraham, as well as Isaac and Jacob, sitting at the table, was idealized as a goal for which to strive.

God of Abraham, God of Isaac, and God of Jacob

This use of the name Abraham is found in the Jewish Bible itself. For example, in Ex. 3:6, when God addresses Moses, God self-identifies in this fashion. Jewish liturgy abounds with this phrase.

The New Testament contains several uses of Abraham's name in such a formula: Mk. 12:26, Mt. 22:32 and Lk. 20:37. The phrase is used semantically to prove that resurrection is a genuine phenomenon. God said to Moses: "I am the God of Abraham. . ." Chronologically, according to the Bible, Abraham, Isaac, and Jacob were already dead. If God is presently their God, then they must have been resurrected for God is God of the living. Acts 7:32 has a similar reference.

In Acts 3:13ff., we find another reference to the God of Abraham, God of Isaac and God of Jacob. After Jesus performs an exorcism and heals a lame man, the crowd is in a state of disbelief. Peter attributes Jesus' power in doing this to the God of Abraham and of Isaac and of Jacob. Because of the proximity of the use of this phrase to the magical act of exorcism, M. Rist sees this incident as supportive of his general hypothesis of a close relationship between the liturgical and magical use of the patriarchal formula "God of Abraham, Isaac, and Jacob."[19] He maintains that there is a connection between the efficacy of the formula and the divine favor which the patriarchs received. An example of this use of Abraham, Isaac and Jacob is found in I Kings 18 where Elijah uses a variation of the formula in his contest on Mt. Carmel. The case of Peter, here in Acts 3:13ff., is another example.

Abraham as the Perfect Proselyte

According to the Rabbinic view, Abraham was the first "convert" to Judaism, and naturally should have proven useful to Paul in convincing the gentile world to embrace Christianity. However, Paul encounters a problem here: circumcision is considered by Scripture to be the perfecting seal of the conversion. Paul's antinomianism prevents him from accepting that element of Abraham's conversion. He denies its significance.

Paul separates the act of circumcision from righteousness itself. Righteousness is not visible. "The outward mark does not create righteousness, but only calls attention to its existence."[20] Thus, circumcision becomes a pointer just as physical descent from Abraham is a pointer. The danger lies in making the pointers ends in themselves. These pointers can only lead to real faith through Jesus.[21]

Rabbinic tradition provides us with the concept that there is no chronology in the Bible. Guided by such an assumption, the Rabbis claim that Abraham performed the whole law before it was given. They base this understanding on Gen. 26:5 where it says that

"Abraham obeyed my voice and kept my charge, my commandments, my statutes, and my laws." This approach runs contrary to Paul's way of thinking. Paul would like to deemphasize the legal responsibility of the believer and thus, in Gal. 3:6f. and Rom. 4:1f., points to Gen. 15:6 which says that Abraham believed in the Lord, and it counted as righteousness. Paul maintains that Abraham was already a convert and righteous before the circumcision took place. Therefore, it is obvious that the circumcision is merely a pointer to a situation that already exists. Abraham may very well have performed works and observed laws, but he was justified by faith before works.[22]

Paul can thus adopt the two notions of Abraham: as the father of the Israelites and as the first of the proselytes. As has already been noted, being a true Israelite did not necessarily depend on mere physical descendancy from Abraham. Here, also, a true proselyte does not necessarily depend solely on the act of circumcision. In both cases, faith is the foremost criterion.[23]

Abraham and Jesus

In John 8:56, Jesus confronts the Jews with the statement that Abraham rejoiced in the hope that Jesus would come. Thus, these Jews are not like Abraham, although they claim to be. They do not accept Jesus, yet Abraham somehow "saw Christ, and was justified, like all Christians, through faith in Christ."[24] Exactly what Jesus is referring to when he claims that Abraham rejoiced is open to speculation.

Lindars accepts what he calls the "common interpretation" that this verse indicates the joy Abraham felt at the birth of Isaac, for it was then that Abraham saw the future Christ eventually fulfilling the promise.[25] Chrysostom's theory (related by Hanson) is that "John 8:56 refers to the sacrifice of Isaac. Abraham recognized in the type of the sacrifice of the ram Christ's self-offering which was to come."[26] Hanson also points out that there is a Rabbinic tradition which claims that, when Abraham is described as "advanced in age" (Gen. 18:9), it means that he entered into the ages to come. Hanson concludes that Abraham would therefore have seen Christ. Hanson further speculates that one of the three angels who visited Abraham in this episode was Christ himself, for in 18:3 Abraham calls one angel "my Lord."[27]

A similar phrase, "advanced in years," occurs in Gen. 24:1 in describing Abraham. Tasker explains that when Abraham makes a covenant with God, it was then that Abraham received a vision of the messianic age. It is the clue given in Gen. 24:1 which is the basis for John's assumption in 8:56.[28] It is reasonable to assume that any or all of these Genesis references could have been an important influence in this Johannine quotation.

Sarah[1]

Sarah is portrayed in the New Testament in two roles, as mother and as wife. In Rom. 9, an example of the "children of the promise" concept includes Sarah as mother of Isaac. In Heb. 11, Sarah is included in the "roll call" for her association with this same event, the birth of a child in her old age. Because she had faith in the promise that was made to her, she did, in fact, conceive. Without her faith, that would not have occurred.[2] Apparently, the writer to the Hebrews ignored her laughter response to the prediction.

In Rom. 4:19, Sarah is recalled as having a barren womb, a problem that Abraham faced and conquered with faith. In I Pet. 3, women are exhorted to be submissive to their husbands as Sarah was to Abraham, showing her obedience by calling him "lord." This exhortation is very similar to the one in I Tim., wherein Eve and Adam are cited as the ideal marriage.

David

The concept of Messiah is derived from the Hebrew word which merely means to anoint someone, usually for a position of importance, such as the kingship or priesthood. The word's first association with David is in I Sam. 16:1-13, wherein David becomes the anointed king. Later, in II Sam. 7:8-16, David is told that, although he will not be permitted to build God's Temple, the Davidic throne will stand forever. The theme of Davidic perpetuity is continued and developed through the Psalms, especially 2, 89 and 110. During the Exile, the hope develops that the great ruler of the future would be descended from David.[1] The Apocryphal books also affirm the eternity of the house of David. The Qumran community expected two messiahs to arise, one of which was to be of the Davidic line.[2]

The idea of the Davidic messiah clearly pervades much New Testament literature. Given the popular notion that a messiah would have to be a descendant of David, it is only natural that "the interest of New Testament writers in David is confined almost exclusively to his relation to Jesus as His ancestor and type."[3]

In any case, the genealogical connection between Jesus and David was more an issue of faith than history.[4] Because faith in Jesus' messiahship is demanded a priori, the issue of Davidic ancestry arises. The writers of the New Testament realized that it was incumbent upon them to believe that Jesus was descended from David and, therefore, presented him in that light.

The genealogies that traced Jesus to David were probably included to answer the Jews' question about the legitimacy of Jesus' claim to the messiahship. In the same manner, the virgin birth stories were included to deal with the similar demands of the gentiles. While Jews insisted on Davidic ancestry for consideration as a "messiah candidate," the pagans associated miraculous birth stories with their divine heroes.

One of the most popular problems in Gospel criticism involves the incompatibility of these two traditions. Since Jesus is traced to David through Joseph, then Jesus could not be born of a virgin. If he was virgin born, then Joseph could have nothing to do with Jesus' genetic components. In the book of James, a later compilation, the Davidic ancestry is traced through Mary, thus indicating that the problem was recognized even then. D. L. Cooper attempts to solve the problem by claiming that Joseph was the foster father of Jesus. "On account of this relationship, Jesus was legally the heir to the throne."[5] Most likely, both traditions, Davidic ancestry and virgin birth, were included as religious statements affirming Jesus' messiahship and divinity, saying, "yes Jesus is the messiah." They were merely directed at two different audiences.

The genealogies of Matthew and Luke also seem to be directed at different audiences for they are written with different purposes in mind. The opening line of Matthew's Gospel is "the book of the genealogy of Jesus Christ, the son of David, the son of Abraham." David is one of the pivotal points of the list, along with Abraham, the Babylonian Exile, and Jesus himself. In addition, many of the Davidic kings are mentioned in this genealogy.

Most of those names are absent from the Lukan genealogy. In fact, it is obvious that Luke had a different source for his list or at least a different interest in the value of the connection to David. The genealogy, which comes in the third chapter, includes David only as another link, like Abraham. Luke wanted to universalize Jesus, tracing him to Adam, the progenitor of the human race. Such particularistic symbols as David and Abraham were inappropriate.

Nevertheless, there are other indications in the Gospels that Jesus' importance was enhanced by his association with David. The healing of Bartimaeus, a blind beggar, involves the use of the phrase "son of David" as an appellation for Jesus (Mk. 10:47-48, Mt. 20:30, Lk. 18:38). In Mt. 5:22, a woman, asking for a miraculous favor, calls Jesus "son of David." When Jesus enters Jerusalem, the crowd welcomes him cheerfully, identifying him with David (Mk. 11:10, Mt. 21:9, 15). In these cases, his primary title seems to be "son of David."

Even when David is not mentioned, there is a possibility that he plays a role in the minds of the New Testament writers. The city of Bethlehem is a reminder of David's birthplace. When that city is named in Mt. 2:5-6, Lk. 2:4, 11, and Jn. 7:42, one can hardly ignore the Davidic association.

As evidenced previously, Matthew seems to emphasize Jesus' association with David. Gundry suggests several implicit parallels in the First Gospel: 2:1f. says that Jesus received worship from the east and 2:11 explains that he received tribute from the gentiles, paralleling similar experiences in David's life.[6] Jesus is also associated with David by the use of antithetic typology, wherein they are placed in similar situations with contrasting results. Mt. 21:14 describes Jesus welcoming the blind and the lame to the Temple where he cures them. When faced with a similar situation in II Sam. 5:8, David rejected the blind and the lame. Thus, by comparison, Jesus emerges as a more compassionate, superior personage.

The tradition associating Jesus with David apparently was known to Paul, too. In his letter to the Romans, Paul begins with "his Son, who was descended from David according to the flesh. . ." However, references to Jesus' descent from David are rare in Pauline literature. For Paul, it is Christ's divinity that is central. The flesh relationship relates better to the portrayal of the humanity of Jesus. In addition, Tyson points out that Paul did not regard accepting Davidic ancestry as essential for Christian faith.[7] Tyson suggests that when the gentiles heard this Jewish messianic association, they did not understand, and so Jesus became the son of God rather than the son of David.[8] Still, Jesus' link to David pervades more books of the New Testament than his identification with any other Tanakhic personage. Indeed, the label "son of David" appears in all four Gospels: Mt. 1:1, Mk. 10:47, Lk. 2:4, Jn. 7:42. Acts 2:30 supports the belief that it was in the Jerusalem form of the kerygma, the early Christian proclamation. II Tim. 2:8 calls Jesus a descendant of David. Revelation 3:7, 5:5, and 22:16 also have Jesus calling himself the "root and offspring of David."

One of the advantages accruing from this association is that the Psalms, which were understood as written by David, could now be "usurped" by the New Testament writers and ascribed to Jesus. In many of the Psalms, David is not only the author but the subject. In some he is praised for his royalty. In others, he is guaranteed an everlasting priesthood. J. W. Doeve points out that once David is acknowledged as the ancestor of Jesus, the Psalms can easily be "hermeneutically" applied to Jesus. "David really did die; so these texts cannot have referred to him; they must refer to Jesus."[9]

There is a simultaneous attempt in the New Testament to curb the association, to soften the typology. The popular concept of the Davidic messiahship had significant political overtones. His role was to restore the glory of Judea.[10] One of the major reasons for the great veneration for the seed of David was the fact that as long as the Davidic dynasty was in control, the Jews had political control over their land.[11] During Jesus' time, there was a significant number of Jews who desired to regain that control, to overthrow Rome. According to Josephus, the most popular type of messianism for these Jews was the "son of David" kind which was associated with a "nostalgic yearning" for the glory of David's reign.[12]

81

The early Christians felt the negative effects of associating Jesus with the son of David. From the time of Vespasian, there was a Roman effort to destroy any hope of a revival of the Davidic dynasty.[13] Jesus' family in Jerusalem had to flee because of the Roman decree ordering the execution of all members of the Davidic line. Later, in 107 C.E., Simon bar Clopas, a Jewish Christian leader, was executed by the Romans because he was a descendant of David.[14]

The New Testament writers tried to tone down the political emphasis of the Davidic ancestry of Jesus. Although such passages as Mk. 11:1-19, wherein Jesus enters Jerusalem to scourge the Temple, are politically powerful, such other passages as Mk. 12:35, 15:2, Jn. 11:47-50, tend to temper that impression by having Jesus deny any understanding of himself as a David successor. Perhaps these passages were designed to balance any political misunderstanding. Thus, there is an ambivalence in the New Testament about Jesus' relation to David.

Jesus' own words contain a denial of the title "son of David." Mk. 12:35-37a, Mt. 22:41-46, and Lk. 20:41-44, contain a semantic game which Jesus plays with the scribes. He uses Ps. 110 to show that he is David's lord and therefore could not be his son. Would a father call his son "Lord"? Jesus seems to want to deny his association as "the son of David." Rather, he emerges as a superior, the same relationship he has to other Tanakhic personages. Implied in this pericope is the chronological priority of the Davidic association with the Messiah. Jesus' denial of such a relationship assumes there was already such a tradition, but that he disagreed with its validity.

There are several places in the Gospels which could have reflected a stronger identification of Jesus with David, but did not. For example, of all the Tanakhic personages, David belonged in the transfiguration scene. Jesus' transfiguration had kingly connotations, yet did not include the greatest of all Israelite kings. Spivey and Smith conclude that this was possibly done to prevent any political misunderstanding.[15]

The Gospel According to John deals almost exclusively with the divinity of Jesus and thus any human association of Jesus with a mortal figure such as David would be out of place. As Glasson points out, John makes little reference to Jesus as the son of David, for his kingdom is not of this world.[16] Meeks concurs that the political element of Davidic ideology is denied by John.[17] In John 11:47-50 is a comment showing the danger of political association of Jesus. It would mean Rome's suspicion and the eventual death of Jesus.

John chooses to concentrate on a different definition of the David/Jesus relationship. In the Bible, David is painted as the shepherd.[18] Ezekiel described God's promise of a shepherd in the Davidic line, a messianic figure. Kee, Young, and Froehlich suggest that Jn. 10's allusion to Jesus as the shepherd is an implicit connection of Jesus with David,[19] an acceptable relationship for John.

Jesus and David have another important connection. Jesus' ideas as professed in his parables and teachings were drawn "largely from the great religious thinkers of his own race," especially the prophets and the Psalmist.[20] The New Testament writers apparently accepted the popular notion that David was the author of the Psalms for they continually use David's name as a synonym for the Psalter, e.g., Mk. 12:36, Acts 1:16, 2:25, 2:34, 4:25, Rom. 4:6, 11:9, Heb. 4:7. Shires believes that Psalms is the most important book of the Bible in New Testament usage.[21]

In Heb. 4, Ps. 89 is recalled to show that David finally brought the "rest" to Israel, a rest which was expected in the days of Joshua.[22] Hanson points out that the emphasis by the writer of Hebrews on the word "today" indicated that Jesus' time is meant as the time when the real rest occurs.[23] Thus, David, as quoted here, is speaking about Jesus, and Jesus takes David's place as the person who inevitably brings "rest" to Israel. In another chapter of Hebrews, 11:32, David is included in the "roll call" of Jewish Biblical heroes who exemplified faith. It was his faith which enabled David to conquer kingdoms.

In Stephen's speech (Acts 7), David is spoken of as the historical figure who initiated the change of tent to Temple as the place where God is worshipped. Stephen speaks mockingly of David's suggestion for it contains a mistaken theological notion: God as dwelling in the tent or sanctuary. God, Stephen points out, does not dwell in houses.

An implicit reference to David in his encounter with Nathan is contained in II Cor. 6:18. In this section of the letter, Paul uses four

83

quotations from Scripture, the last of which is part of Nathan's rebuke to David, telling him that one of his seed will have the privilege of building the Temple, a privilege denied to David himself. The incident, according to Tasker,[24] is used by Paul to explain that it is Christ to whom Nathan is referring. It is not Solomon's Temple, nor the Temple of the Second Commonwealth, but the Temple made up of believing Christians that will be the dwelling place of God.

After Jesus is accused of profaning the Sabbath (Mk. 2:23-28, Mt. 12:1-9, Lk. 6:3), he responds by citing an incident in David's life. Jesus was being castigated for allowing his disciples to pick ears of grain on the Sabbath. Jesus refers to I Sam. 21:1-6, wherein David breaks a law by eating the sacred shewbread. Jesus explains that the case of David set a precedent for need prevailing over the law. His disciples, too, were hungry. Anderson points out that the New Testament uses a normal Rabbinic argument of "minor to major" (Kal vahomer) to show that if David could transgress the law, so much more so could Jesus.[25] Tasker explains that, "of all the characters in the Old Testament, David is the most conspicuous type of the Messiah who was to be born of his lineage. If David then could 'defile' the Sabbath and be guiltless, how much more could He do so who inaugurated that divine reign of which the reign of David was but a foretaste."[26]

The number of explicit citations of David in the New Testament, almost equalling those of Moses or Abraham, is illusory. One would expect to find him used for many different exegetical and theological purposes as Moses and Abraham were. Instead, we find that David was mentioned almost exclusively as the ancestor and type for Jesus.

Elijah (and Elisha)

In the Bible, Elijah is a miracle-working prophet who, like his successor, Elisha, performs wonders and signs to prove to people that he is speaking for God. In Jewish tradition, the figure of Elijah elicits warm feelings of hope. At the Passover Seder, an extra cup of wine is poured for him in anticipation of his expected visit, his return to earth to announce the coming of the messiah. This tradition probably has its roots in Mal. 4:5, where he is described as coming before "the great and terrible day of the Lord." The fact that Elijah's death is not recorded in Scripture, which contains instead a description of Elijah's ascension to God, is in part also responsible for the development of the idea of his return.

Elijah is also understood as a messiah figure in his own right. Not merely a forerunner, Elijah is seen as the prophet-king himself who will solve all the problems of the world and bring peace to mankind. Teeple believes that this tradition was so strong that the similar Mosaic traditions were modeled after Elijah.[1] In any case, Elijah is seen as a link in the messianic chain, if not the messiah himself.

This apparent confusion over the exact nature of Elijah's role is also reflected in the New Testament's presentation of him. He is, in some places, identified with John the Baptist, in others, with Jesus and in still another, with Paul. As we examine the various contexts in which Elijah appears, it should become understandable why this ambiguity occurs.

Elijah and John the Baptist
It is quite apparent that John the Baptist is presented as the forerunner of Jesus in the Gospels. The stage is set for this identification by the opening passage of the Gospel of Mark, which tells us that God has sent a messenger to "prepare the way" for the Lord; in the next verse, John the Baptist appears. The Gospel of Luke is even more explicit, for while John the Baptist is still in his mother's womb, the child is described as one who will "make ready for the Lord. . ." Immediately following is a prediction about Jesus who will be born and be called son of God. John the Baptist himself tells the crowd that there is one coming after who is greater than he (Mt. 3:11, Mk. 1:7, Lk. 3:16). It is clear that the Synoptic Gospels identify John the Baptist as a predecessor to the messiah.

Luke identifies Elijah as that forerunner, naming Elijah in Lk. 1:17 as the model for John the Baptist: "He will go before him in the spirit and power of Elijah."

Robinson suggests that John the Baptist believed that Elijah was the messiah, not the forerunner, and so regarded Elijah as the one to come after him. Robinson explains that there is no pre-Christian evidence that Elijah was considered the forerunner of the messiah, but rather, that this notion arose during the church's development. Mal. 4:5 says that Elijah will come before "the great and terrible day of the Lord," but says nothing of his coming before a messiah.[2]

Robinson feels that even the writers of the Gospels did not believe that John the Baptist was Elijah. A later editor added glosses to create this parallel: e.g., the opening of Mark's Gospel. John the Baptist's preaching, which led people to believe that Elijah would come after him, was apparently so successful that they mistook Jesus for Elijah (Mt. 16:14, Mk. 8:27f., Lk. 9:18f.). Robinson also points out John the Baptist's association with water, in contrast to Elijah, who is associated with fire.[3] Jn. 1:21 is the most convincing argument of all, for when John the Baptist is asked if he is Elijah, he says no! Robinson feels that the association of Elijah with John the Baptist came after the Gospels were written.

That view is in consonance with Teeple's contention that Elijah's role of leading the people to repentance developed as a consequence of his association with John the Baptist.[4] Thus, the typological direction seems to point from John the Baptist to Elijah rather than the opposite.

Nevertheless, the Gospels possibly reflect an image of John the Baptist as an Elijah figure in other ways. For instance, John the Baptist is "clothed with camel's hair, and had a leather girdle around his waist, and ate locusts and honey" (Mk. 1:6, Mt. 3:4), a description similar to that of Elijah in II Kgs. 1:8. Robinson, however, points to Zech. 13:4, which implies that anyone wishing to be taken for a prophet would attire himself in that manner; "there is no suggestion that its wearer was intended to be identified specifically with Elijah.[5]

Another example is the suggestion that the description of Herod and Herodias' execution of John the Baptist (Mk. 6:14-29, Mt. 1-12, Lk. 9:7-9) was modeled after Ahab and Jezebel's hatred for Elijah and their desire for such a murder (I Kgs. 19). However, Tasker argues that it is impossible to prove that assumption.[6]

The clearest and most authoritative identification of John the Baptist with Elijah is when Jesus himself verbalizes the connection. In Mt. 11:14, Jesus explicitly names John the Baptist as Elijah. Following the transfiguration scene, wherein Moses and Elijah appear with Jesus on the mountain, Jesus tells his disciples that John the Baptist is Elijah in answer to their apparent concern about what part John the Baptist plays in the overall events. Anderson believes that they are alluding to Mal. 4:5.[7] Thus, Jesus identifies John the Baptist as Elijah to show them that Elijah has already come. According to Teeple, Jesus made this identification in response to the objections of the Pharisees that Jesus could not be the Messiah since Elijah had not yet come as predicted.[8]

The central problem of the identification of John the Baptist with Elijah lies in the origin of the concept of Elijah as forerunner. This is apparently a post-Biblical tradition and it is impossible to know how much responsibility lies in the Apocrypha, in Rabbinic literature, or in the developing church. It is clear, however, that John the Baptist is seen as Elijah in many different passages of the Gospels, as not only the forerunner of Jesus, but as a link between the Scriptures and the New Testament.

Elijah and Jesus
Jesus, too, is identified as Elijah in several places, although not as frequently as John the Baptist. Meeks ascribes the infrequency to the fact that the typology was already applied to John the Baptist and could therefore be too confusing to the readers.[9]

M. Enslin claims that John the Baptist was Jesus' rival as a messianic figure.[10] The New Testament writers therefore appropriated John the Baptist as one of their own personages because his following was substantial. By presenting John the Baptist in a subordinate role to Jesus, the Gospel writers manage to unite two factions which were historically in competition for disciples. A possible confusion over which was the authentic messiah could have led to the identification of both of them with Elijah in his role as messiah, and this may have inadvertently been reflected in the Gospels. On the other hand, the Gospels' depiction of John the Baptist as Elijah in his role as forerunner serves the purpose of subordinating the Baptist to Jesus. Furthermore, John the Baptist could not be the messiah since he was not descended from David. Therefore, the writers of the Gospels themselves could have differentiated the roles of Elijah, casting John the Baptist as forerunner and Jesus as messiah, for Jesus, too, is identified with Elijah.

According to Mal. 4:6 and apocryphal sources (Eccles. 48:10, II Esd. 6:26), Elijah is to bring peace to the earth; he is to settle all disputes.[11] Robinson suggests that Jesus is identified with Elijah in this capacity in Lk. 12:51, where Jesus asks, "Do you think that I have come to give peace on earth?"

When Herod hears about Jesus, he is confused. He thinks that either John the Baptist has risen from the dead or Elijah has appeared (Mk. 6, Mt. 14, Lk. 9:8). These passages at once confirm the fact that Jesus and John the Baptist may have been mistaken for each other and that both were identified with Elijah. When Jesus asks his disciples about his identity among the people, he is told that some think he is Elijah, while others think he is John the Baptist.

Teeple suggests three explanations for Jesus' identification with Elijah. First of all, there was a strong belief that Jesus was both a prophet and messiah. Elijah was viewed similarly, especially in Jesus' time. Secondly, like Elijah, Jesus spent forty days in the wilderness without food. Thirdly, they both preached that the eschatological kingdom of God and judgment day were about to appear.[12] Robinson postulates that Jesus himself saw his role in John the Baptist's terms, as Elijah. While it is true that Jesus was to be the Christ, he was first supposed to be Elijah.[13]

In the transfiguration scene, Jesus is flanked by Moses and Elijah. A Jewish tradition explains that both Moses and Elijah would return as forerunners of the messiah. This, according to Glasson, was such a popular belief that it influenced the writing of the transfiguration scene and Revelation 11, wherein two anonymous figures are apparently Moses and Elijah.[14] Teeple feels that Rev. 11 is the union of two rivaling concepts of the messiah's identity, Moses and Elijah. It is apparent that the two figures in Rev. 11:6 are colored by Moses as he appears in Ex. 7, 17, and 19, and Elijah in II Kgs. 1:10 and I Kgs. 17:1. As already pointed out, Teeple suggests that the major reason Moses even appears as a returning messiah figure was the tradition that Elijah would return. Moses was, after all, the greatest of the prophets, and could surely do what Elijah could.[15] Meeks suggests that there were two equally important strands in eschatological expectation: one of Elijah as depicted in Mal. 3:1, the other of Moses as depicted in Deut. 18:15.[16]

Spivey and Smith believe that Moses and Elijah appear in the transfiguration scene because they too are associated with significant events on mountains.[17] Kee, Young, and Froehlich feel that Moses represents the Law, the first unit of the Bible; while Elijah represents the prophets, the second unit. Thus, Jesus has the sanction of the two most important parts of the Bible.[18]

Although Elijah represents the other prophets, there is a significant difference between them. The latter prophets are known for their role as rebukers of the people. They are not magicians, nor even predictors of the seemingly unpredictable. However, Elijah, like Elisha, his successor, is a miracle-working prophet, living in an unsophisticated world and society. The people they confront demand signs as proof of their authority.

H. Baumgard believes that Jesus, too, did much of his work in that kind of area, the Galilee, which by contrast to Jerusalem and the south, was less "urbanized" and less "sophisticated". In addition, the people were living under terrible Roman oppression; they were therefore less inclined to accept a rationalistic religion, and were naturally more attracted to pay heed to a person who could produce miracles. Baumgard claims that this is one of the reasons that the New Testament writers reported the various miracles of Jesus.[19] These miracles are extremely reminiscent of those performed by Elijah and Elisha. However, as Baumgard points out, these miracles were beheld by Jesus' followers as signs of divinity, while Elijah and Elisha performed the same as "ordinary workings" of their mission, and remained human beings.[20]

TABLE IV

Parallel Miracles of Jesus and Elijah/Elisha

Jesus	Elijah/Elisha
Walking on water:	Dividing water and walking through:
Mt. 14:22-33	II Kgs. 2:8
Mk. 6:45-52	II Kgs. 2:14

89

Jesus	Elijah/Elisha
Feeding multitudes:	Feeding multitudes and replenishing
Mt. 14:13-21	diminished oil:
Mt. 15:32-39	II Kgs. 4:42-44
Mk. 8:1-10	II Kgs. 4:1ff.
Mk. 6:30-44	
Lk. 9:10-17	
Lk. 2:1-11	
Healing:	Healing:[21]
Mt. 8:1-4	II Kgs. 5:1-14
Mt. 9:1-8	II Kgs. 4:25-37
Mt. 9:27-31	I Kgs. 17:17-24
Mt. 20:29-34	II Kgs. 13:20-21
Mk. 1:40-45	
Mk. 2:1-12	
Mk. 10:46-52	
Lk. 5:12-16	
Lk. 5:17-26	
Lk. 18:35-43	

Luke's use of the miracles has an interesting additional significance. Elijah and Elisha are singled out in Lk. 4:23f. as prophets who performed their wonders for the gentiles at a time when there were yet many Jews who needed aid. There were many Jewish widows during Elijah's time, yet he grants his powers to helping a foreign widow. There were many lepers during Elisha's day, yet it is Naaman the gentile who is cleansed by the Jewish prophet. Elijah and Elisha, through these acts, symbolize the universalistic mission that is so important in Luke's writings. In fact, Lindars claims that I and II Kings, which contain the history of these two prophets, is used throughout Luke for typology even though no explicit quotations are cited.[22]

Both Lk. 12:49-53 and Jn. 4:4 contain a reference to Jesus as one who brings fire to the earth. While John the Baptist is associated with his baptismal water, Jesus and Elijah were both men of fire. Elijah's most famous wonder is associated with the fire on Mt. Carmel (I Kgs. 18:38).[23]

90

The miraculous nature of their deaths is another parallel of Jesus and Elijah/Elisha. The Biblical prophets were not resurrected but their deaths are shrouded in mystery. Elisha's bones had the magical power to resurrect life in a dead body that touched them. Elijah was gathered up in a whirlwind to the heavens. This led to the mysterious legends of his future return. It is no wonder that Jesus, who, to believing Christians, was the son of God and descended to the earth to bring salvation to humanity, would be identified with Elijah. Since Elijah had never died, then someone like Elijah could be Elijah.[24] Jesus' similarities to the prophet would lead to the belief that he was Elijah returned. Another parallel in their "deaths" is the rending of material. When Elijah is carried up to heaven, Elisha rips his garment in mourning. Immediately following Jesus' Crucifixion, the curtain in the Temple is ripped.

When Jesus is on the cross, he begins to recite Ps. 22, saying "Eli, Eli (My God, my God)." The people standing nearby apparently did not understand Jesus' reference to the Psalms and mistakenly think that he is calling for Elijah since his name sounds similar to the opening word of the Psalm. They mockingly ask whether Elijah will come to help. They may also have been mocking Jesus' claim that the messianic era was about to begin. They could have been thinking that Elijah would therefore be due to arrive, and been wondering aloud why he was not there. This passage certainly assumes that the crowd did not regard Jesus as Elijah, for if he were, then how could Elijah come to help?

Elijah and Paul
Paul identifies himself with Elijah in Rom. 11:2, when he says that Elijah, like himself, was rejected by the majority of his people. But just as God did not abandon the chosen people during Elijah's time, neither will God forsake Paul and the remnant that follow him.[25]

Thus, there are many ways in which Elijah is depicted in New Testament writings. He has the outstanding distinction of serving as the type for three key figures, John the Baptist, Jesus, and Paul.

Naaman[1]

In the Bible, Naaman is a gentile who comes to Elisha to be healed of his leprosy. The instructions Naaman receives are faithfully carried out, resulting in the cure of his problem. Thus, Naaman is a perfect example of a gentile receiving redemption from a Hebrew prophet. This message is clearly one of universalism, appropriate for Luke's Gospel, where, in 4:27, Luke uses Naaman, along with the gentile woman who receives aid from Elijah, as examples of gentiles who were willing and eager to receive divine redemption. "If God's grace can evoke no response of faith in Israel, it will turn to the Gentiles."[2]

Jacob (and Rebecca)

Although he is mentioned twenty-four times in the New Testament, his significance is not worthy of major note. Most of the references to him (sixteen) are within genealogies or in the phrase, "God of Abraham, Isaac, and Jacob."

In Jn. 4, Jesus is shown to be greater than Jacob. The water that Jesus gives will quench the thirst of everyone who drinks, while those who drink of the water of Jacob's well "will thirst again."

In Stephen's speech, Acts 7, Jacob plays a part in the recounting of history. Even there, he is more important as Joseph's father than as a personage himself.

In Rom. 9, Jacob is mentioned in opposition to Esau. Although both are sons of Isaac, only one receives the blessing, thus illustrating the theological issue of God's grace. Paul intends to show the reader that God is only merciful to whom God chooses. Although Esau may have the right to expect good favor, he received none. Jacob, on the other hand, was chosen by God to be rewarded.[1]

Finally, in Heb. 11, Jacob appears in the roll call of faithful heroes, showing his faith in the future by worshipping God through blessing his grandchildren. J. H. Davies points out that the use of "the rod of Jacob" is out of place. In the Biblical account, Jacob leans on the rod in the story preceding the blessing of these children.[2] Hanson suggests that the "rod of Jacob" possibly foreshadows Jesus' cross.[3]

Esau[1]

Besides being mentioned in opposition to Jacob in Rom. 9, Esau is also cited in Heb. 11. He is not one who himself exhibited faith but was a vehicle through which Isaac showed faith by blessing his sons with hope for the future.

In Heb. 12, Esau is recalled in a negative light when he is called immoral and irreligious for selling his birthright. Christians are exhorted not to give up faith as quickly as Esau did when he gave in to Jacob too easily, and as a result, lost both his birthright and his blessing. The writer of Hebrews is possibly writing to a group of people who may be close to apostasy, warning them that, by giving up their "Christian sonship," they will, like Esau, lose their blessing, "their heavenly salvation."[2]

Isaac (and Hagar)

The name of Isaac appears but twenty times in the New Testament, yet his influence is possibly even more pervasive. Besides being mentioned for genealogical purposes and in the phrase "Abraham, Isaac, and Jacob," Isaac is associated with several Biblical incidents that were recalled by New Testament writers.

In Luke's genealogy, Isaac is merely another name, one of many which come as insignificant links in a chain that receives attention only on its two ends, Adam and Jesus. Since Isaac has no universalistic significance, a greater role for him in the genealogy would not have served Luke's purposes.

Matthew's list of names begins with Abraham. Thus, Isaac, his son, has the distinguished honor of being the second name in a list which focuses on the Jewish origin of Jesus. This could be considered support for the argument that Matthew was a Jewish Christian or was writing for such an audience. It would then seem natural that he would grant more emphasis to Isaac, along with others of the Abrahamic line, who formed the means through which the glory of

God passed to Jesus himself, maintaining the continuity of Jewish history.

Isaac's historical position as the link between Abraham and Jacob is also the reason he is mentioned in the phrase "God of Abraham, Isaac, and Jacob"[1] and other similar expressions throughout the New Testament. Some of those instances are found in Mt. 8:11, 22:32, Mk. 12:26, Lk. 13:28, 20:37, Acts 3:13, and 7:32. In Acts 7:8, he is mentioned only as the object of the circumcision; he is acted upon. His role as a personage, acting in his own right, is not given very much consideration.

In Heb. 11, the "roll call of Biblical heroes," Isaac is mentioned five times. He, along with Abraham and Jacob, lived in tents; he was offered up in the Akedah; he was the vehicle through which Abraham was blessed; he was figuratively resurrected; he had enough faith in the future to grant blessings to his children. Davidson feels that, even here, Isaac is only a minor character for the writer of Hebrews, for Isaac is still the object or vehicle for Abraham, and not an active subject himself.[2] Isaac's significance is minimized even more when one considers the large number of heroes and incidents that are included in Heb. 11. A. T. Hanson, however, feels that great consideration should be given to Isaac's appearance in Heb. 11:19. Isaac is a type of the resurrection, given back to his father after Abraham thought that he would have to kill him.[3]

The mention of Isaac in Jas. 2:21 is another example of James' argument that works are as significant as faith. Abraham did not just believe in God; he engaged in substantive action, taking his son to sacrifice him. Here is an example of works, of action. Once again, however, Isaac is the object, not the subject.

In Pauline literature, we have some indication that Isaac played a greater role. In Gal. 4, an allegory establishes a contrast between Hagar and Ishmael, on the one hand, and Sarah and Isaac, on the other. Abraham had two sons: Ishmael, born of a slave, Hagar; and Isaac, born of a free woman, Sarah. Ishmael's birth is associated with Mt. Sinai, reminiscent of the old covenant, where the Mosaic law was given. His birth was "after the flesh." On the other hand, Isaac's extraordinary birth was "out of nature." He belongs to "Jerusalem above" and symbolizes the "children of the promise."[4] We recall that

Abraham, in many instances, represents the Jewish people.[5] Here, Isaac represents the Christian people, interpreted by Paul to be the "children of the promise."

This allegory is, of course, very complicated and has many failings. R. P. C. Hanson believes it is an "unconvincing allegory, not easily worked out, because one is uncertain how far Paul is allegorizing Ishmael and how far Hagar, and whether he is not in fact confusing the two allegories, and because he hardly works out at all the other allegory of Isaac and Sarah."[6] However, Hanson still feels there are definite equations made here. "The rejection by God of the Jewish race as the exclusive object of his choice is allegorically prefigured in Hagar."[7]

Paul also clearly meant to equate Isaac with the first century Christians as the "children of the promise." R. Rosenberg points out that this equation is previously alluded to in Gal. 3:16, wherein Paul mentions that Abraham will have his promise fulfilled through one offspring, apparently Isaac.[8] Another implication of Paul's comparison of Sarah and Hagar, symbols of freedom and slavery, is that Christians are born free, not enslaved to the law.

In Rom. 9, Isaac once again represents the "children of the promise." An old theme is reiterated: physical descent is not as important as spiritual descent.[9] Isaac was the result and inheritor of God's promise to Abraham. He was not just a mere physical descendant, as was Ishmael in Paul's allegory. The true descent is, therefore, not merely physical. Although all Israelites are physical descendants, they are not necessarily heirs of the promise.[10]

Thus, in Paul's writing, too, we have no explicit development of Isaac/Jesus typology. For Paul, the key event in Isaac's life seems to be the prediction to Abraham that Isaac would be born. Both Rom. 9 and Gal. 4 associate the Christians as "children of the promise" with Isaac. Jesus and Isaac are nowhere compared or contrasted.

In Rom. 8:32, however, we have an echo of a Biblical event, the Akedah, in which Isaac plays a greater part. Paul says, "God did not spare his only son." H. Schoeps and J. Hastings are among scholars who feel that "it is just possible" that the binding of Isaac had a great influence on such statements as Rom. 8:32.[11] It would be difficult to deny the influence of Gen. 22.

The parallels between Isaac and Jesus are striking. Both Sarah and Mary are told, much to their surprise, that they will bear Isaac and Jesus respectively. Isaac and Jesus are born under "miraculous" conditions: Sarah is ninety years old; Mary is a virgin. The Akedah is ostensibly the sacrifice of Isaac, Abraham's "only" son. The Crucifixion is the sacrifice of Jesus, God's only son. Isaac, on the way to his death, carries the wood for his sacrifice. Jesus, on the way to his death, carries his cross. Isaac accepts his fate with perfect obedience. He is perfectly silent, not arguing with his father. Jesus offers himself in a similar fashion. He is practically silent when interrogated by the Roman authorities.[12]

When the Midrash is considered, the similarities between the two figures become even more convincing.[13] The Binding of Isaac takes place at Passover, as does the Crucifixion. The association of Passover with death was already popular to some degree because of the plaque condemning the first-born in Egypt.[14] Furthermore, Rosenberg argues that Jesus and his disciples followed the solar-pentecostal calendar, according to which Jesus' death and Isaac's "death" are parallel with regard to the number of Jubilees from the creation of the world.[15]

There are many midrashim wherein Isaac is injured, maimed, or actually killed by Abraham. In some of these midrashim he is butchered. In others, he is burnt. Some of the stories have him resurrected immediately. Others send him off to Paradise or to the school of Shem and Eber to study. One midrash explains that Isaac must have been burnt to death, for he was placed upon the wood, which was already ignited. When his father was forbidden to lay a hand upon him, he was unable to remove him from the flames. Another clever story gives evidence of Isaac's sojourn in Paradise. The next time Isaac is mentioned in Scripture after the Akedah, Rebecca sees him meditating in the field and falls off her camel. The reason for this, the Rabbis explained, is that she was shocked at observing Isaac reentering the world in an upside-down position, as is the custom for those returning from Paradise.[16]

In the Talmud there are several references to the Akedah in association with ashes. In B. Zebachim 62a, Isaac's ashes lay on the spot in Jerusalem where the altar should be.[17] In the Mishna, Taanit XI:3-5, associated with the fast days is a prayer which, according to the Gemara (Tan. 16a) was understood as an expiation in connection with the strewing of ashes on the head.[18] S. Spiegel says that the ashes are symbolic of Isaac's ashes, giving testimony that Isaac is actually offered up.[19]

Zlotowitz suggests that the Rabbis selected Gen. 22, along with other high holiday readings, as a polemic against Christianity precisely because there are so many parallels between the Binding of Isaac and the Crucifixion. The Rabbis could, therefore, show that Jewish tradition contained all the ingredients and more that were found in Christianity.[20] To the Rabbis, Isaac proved to be a greater sacrifice than Jesus, for Abraham's son was without blemish. He remained silent and did not cry out the words of apparent desperation: "O God, why have you forsaken me?" as Jesus did at the Crucifixion. Could this same motive be attributed to New Testament writers in their reporting of the Crucifixion? Could they have wanted to go one better than Judaism by showing that in Jesus' case, the sacrifice is complete, not having been stopped at the last minute like its counterpart in Gen. 22? Why, then, is there not a stronger identification of Jesus with Isaac?

G. Vermes argues strongly in favor of the Rabbinic influence in the New Testament writers. He feels that the Rabbinic traditions associated with the Binding of Isaac were well developed by the first century and therefore would have to have played an important role in the minds of the New Testament writers. Vermes assumes that the New Testament writers were exposed to these traditions. He also assumes an early dating for the Targum, for he points to the two main Targumic themes of the Akedah: Isaac's willingness to be offered, and the atoning value of the sacrifice.[21] Vermes explains that Isaac, in the Targumic version, was able to see the perfection of the heavens, which descended at the time of the Akedah. The transfiguration scene in the New Testament allows Jesus that same privilege.[22] The New Testament writers use similar language to that of Gen. 22. Acts 3:25-26 is reminiscent of Gen. 22:18 and the baptism scene (Mk. 1:11, Mt. 3:17, and Lk. 3:22) uses words borrowed from Gen. 22:16.[23] Vermes contends that Paul used Akedah theology in understanding the Crucifixion. Besides Rom. 8:32, which echoes Gen. 22:16, Gal. 3:6-29 is based on the reading of Gen. 22:12, 18.[24]

Isaac's sacrifice, for the Palestinian Jew of Jesus' time, was "the sacrifice par excellence, whose lasting benefits would be felt for all time."[25] They associated the sacrifice with the salvation of the first-born of Israel at Passover, with the success of the Israelites at the Red Sea, with the preservation of Jerusalem after David took a census, with the pardon of the Israelites after the golden calf, and even with the deliverance of the Jews from Haman.[26] The idea that Jesus dies for the sins of humanity seems more than coincidental with this theme.

Vermes claims a parallel exists between the Eucharist, an everyday reminder of the Crucifixion, and the daily recitation of the Akedah passage in Jewish liturgy.[27] For the Palestinian Jew of the first century, the Temple sacrifices were memorials of the Akedah. The lamb used for the Passover and Tamid offerings were reminiscent of the ram which God provided in place of Isaac. Vermes believes that a parallel relationship underlies the words of Jn. 1:29, where both the lamb and Jesus have the effect of "deliverance, forgiveness of sin, and messianic salvation."[28]

Schoeps also feels strongly that the Rabbinic traditions concerning the Binding of Isaac were early enough to have had an effect on Paul's understanding of Jesus' atoning value. He believes that Rom. 5:9, wherein Paul claims that Jesus' blood justifies the Christians, is based on the assumption that the Binding of Isaac gave similar power to the blood on the doorposts in Egypt.[29] Schoeps cites a study by I. Lévi, who claims the schools of Hillel and Shammai discussed the Akedah as part of the liturgy for the New Year because of the theological implications of the Binding of Isaac, illustrating the expiatory power of the sacrifice.[30]

Other scholars argue that the Akedah was not important to the early Christians and possibly not even to the Jews of that time. Even if the Akedah were important to the Jewish community because of its association with ritual sacrifice and the value of atonement, the early Christians did not focus on these concepts. R. Scroggs feels that the themes of the New Testament do not include the concept of atonement, for, in his view, the people were not terrible sinners who needed it. Paul's exclusive emphasis in the Crucifixion is to show that "Jesus is God - recognize it."[31] The theme that Christ died for the sins of humanity is not important to Paul. In fact, he uses a legal, not sacrificial, metaphor in justifying Jesus' death.[32] Scroggs also points out that none of the Gospels nor Acts focuses on Jesus as atonement.

Barrett is also convinced that the Akedah is not important to Paul. Rom. 4, to Barrett's mind, could not have been written without some explicit reference to the Akedah, if, in fact, the Akedah was significant to Paul. "For him [Paul], the outstanding example of Abraham's faith was not his willingness to sacrifice his son but his confident belief that God would give him and his wife a child, notwithstanding their great age."[33]

The possibility remains that both the Akedah and the Crucifixion are independently based on a third source. Spiegel claims that, during Philo's time, there were critics of Abraham and Isaac who cited other myths of child sacrifice. Philo's effort was to show that the Akedah is different, for it was performed for a different reason that the others.[34] Perhaps the Crucifixion was presented as it was to show that it was different from the pagan myths, that there was a sophisticated theological purpose to such an act.

Rosenberg cites a pagan custom which was adopted by the Israelites in their suffering servant motif. He points to a pagan substitution rite wherein one person dies for the rest of the people. Rosenberg feels that Isaac became the prototype of the suffering servant since he was the first to experience "chastisements" from God in such a fashion. Rosenberg believes that ultimately both the Crucifixion and the Binding of Isaac stem from the Canaanite practice of periodically sacrificing a royal figure for the welfare of the people.[35]

Many questions arise upon examining the role of Isaac in the New Testament. He is certainly one of the most extended Biblical figures in the Midrash, with there perhaps being more fanciful interpretations of what was done to him than to any other personage. The Akedah played a great role in the Rabbinical writings. It is fairly certain that the Binding of Isaac and the Crucifixion served as material for later Jewish-Christian polemics. Zlotowitz feels that the relationship between Jesus' death and the Binding of Isaac is at the core of Jewish-Christian polemics. It is a wonder, therefore, that there is so little explicit mention of Isaac in the New Testament and furthermore, that he does not serve as a type for Jesus.

The possibility remains that the ideas and themes associated with the Binding of Isaac did develop in the minds of the writers of the New Testament. There could very well have been an underlying influence of Isaac on the material that they wrote. They may have purposely wanted to avoid explicit reference in an effort to exclude the possibility of a Jesus/Isaac comparison. The Crucifixion, with its theological implications, was certainly an event which should remain unique to Christianity. Thus, an avoidance of its comparison to any other event may have been deliberate.

Adam

Two of the four non-Pauline explicit references to Adam are genealogical. Luke, in his effort to show the universalistic nature of salvation through Jesus, chooses Adam, the father of the entire human race, over Abraham, the father of the Jewish people, as the source of Jesus' blood line. While either of these patriarchs could be used to illustrate a continuity from the old covenant to the new, that continuity in the Gospel According to Luke extends past Abraham, the particularistic, to Adam, the progenitor of all mankind. Although the Rabbis say that Adam is the first Israelite, tracing his royalty through Seth to Abraham, thereby making Israel the main purpose of God's creation,[1] Luke chooses Adam to dispute that very claim. "Jesus is the world's redeemer, not merely [the redeemer of] the children of Israel."[2]

Adam is used genealogically in Jude 1:14 to historically pinpoint "Enoch in the seventh generation from Adam." Enoch's chronological position is better understood because Adam signifies the beginning of time.

Adam's relationship to Eve is referred to in I Tim. 2:13, 14, as an illustration of what the writer saw as a logical reason for male supremacy. It is only natural that Adam, who was created before Eve (Gen. 2), and who, by contrast to his spouse, was not deceived by the serpent, should dominate his wife.

In the Gospels (Mk. 10:6-8, Mt. 19:4-6), Jesus tells the Pharisees his view on divorce. As a proof-text for "the absolute indissolubility of the marriage tie," Jesus implicitly refers to the union of Adam and

Eve by recalling the creation story.[3] J. H. Davies suggests one other implicit reference to Adam in Heb. 2:11 where the people whom Jesus saves "have all one origin."[4]

Adam is explicitly and implicitly more important to Paul than to any other New Testament writer. Adam, as the first man, is an almost perfect type for Jesus, forming an excellent foundation for the development and explanation of Paul's concepts of sin and redemption, death and resurrection. Ellis says "the Adam-Christ typology provides the scaffolding for his [Paul's] doctrine of redemption and resurrection."[5] and in that typology the "whole scope of cosmic redemption appears to be encompassed."[6]

D. M. Smith believes that the use of Adam by Paul, explicitly in Rom. 5 and I Cor. 15, and implicitly in Phil. 2, II Cor. 5, and Gal. 6, is the first case of typology in the development of the New Testament.[7] The similarity between Jesus and Adam is that they are both "first men" symbolizing whole worlds of people. Adam is, according to the Bible, the first created man, existent before all other humans, so that all who come after him are literally descended from his seed.[8]

For Paul, not only is Adam literally the father of the human race, but he symbolizes every member of that race. Paul's belief that "everything that could be said about Adam. . . could be said about mankind as a whole"[9] echoes the Rabbinic concept that "the 'body' of Adam included all mankind," from any geographical location, whether male or female.[10] Paul sees Christ as an Adamic figure, who also incorporates all of humanity: male and female, Jew and Greek. Jesus is "the second Adam," "the last Adam," "the new Adam," the originator of a new creation, a new race of human.[11] Like the first Adam, Jesus is "the man God intends all men to be."[12] The use of the preposition "in" with their names in Rom. 5:19: "in Adam," "in Christ," conveys the idea that they act not as individuals but on behalf of the human race; their acts affect all humanity.[13] Finally, they are both "the son of God."

However alike they appear to be, their contrasts are even more distinctive. The most obvious difference is that Adam is human, Jesus divine. Even the supernatural myths of the Midrash, such as the one which depicts Adam as the tallest creature in the world, never deifies Adam, while Jesus' divinity is the basis of the New Testament.

For Paul, Adam is the symbol of sin, failing to be what "God intends all men to be." Adam, revealing his vanity, a symbol of the wrong attitude, seeks independence to deal with God as an equal. His disobedience leads to failure to achieve the immortality that is possible for all members of the human race. Christ, on the other hand, accomplishes victory over sin, bringing the requisite acquittal to remove sin's burden. Jesus, in contrast to Adam, remains perfectly obedient to God's will, entering the world with humility, content with being the Son of God.[14] Whereas Adam's failure brings sin and death to all, Christ's victory brings righteousness and immortal life.[15]

Another significant difference is in the contrast between the physical and the spiritual as explained in I Cor. 15. While "First Adam," symbolizing the human's earthly nature, consists of those elements associated with death, such as earth and dust, "Second Adam," symbolizing the human's spiritual nature, brings relief from death by means of immortality and resurrection of the soul. By joining the new spiritual humanity with faith in Christ, one can become immune from the sting of death, as G. B. Stevens says, "the accompaniments of sorrow, pain, and fear."[16]

The influence of Adam is found throughout Paul's writings, as if Paul is continuously conscious of the typology. M. D. Hooker feels that there are many implicit references to Adam such as Rom. 1:23, wherein "Adam [is] not far from Paul's mind,"[17] as indicated by the language, reminiscent of Gen. 1.

There has been much speculation about which source most influences Paul in his understanding of Adam. Surely the Biblical story itself contains the seeds for many of Paul's ideas: disobedience and sin followed by death are self-evident in Genesis. Barrett argues that Paul knew Hebrew and therefore was aware that Adam meant humanity in general and conceptualized that element into his Adam-Christ typology.[18] F. R. Tennant suggests that Paul's concept of Adam was "formed by fusing the first man of Gen. iii with the undifferentiated Adam, or generic man, of Gen. ii."[19] Scroggs also feels that there are two images of Adam taken from the Bible: Adam as bearer of sin and death, and the honored and exalted Adam.[20]

Scroggs argues against the notion that Paul's Adam received direct influence from the gnostic concept of Urmensch, believing instead that Paul's Adam has its roots in both Scripture and the popular Jewish interpretation of the first man. If anything, those elements which were shared by gnostic and Pauline theology are contained in the Jewish theology to which Paul had access.[21] The Midrash,[22] source of Jewish theology, includes many ideas that seem to be incorporated into Paul's notion of Adam. One midrash in particular perhaps provided the framework for Paul's typological concept: six things lost through Adam's fall are to be restored through the Messiah.[23] Stevens,[24] and Spivey and Smith[25] agree that Paul's Adamic concept was most heavily influenced by the Bible and popular Jewish theology.

There are, however, major differences between Paul's concept and those found in the Jewish sources. Scroggs points out that "the rabbis are not interested in making Adam into a savior figure who has a personal involvement in the acts or results of the eschatological events,"[26] while Jesus, of course, fits that description quite well. Ellis also contrasts Paul to the Rabbis with regard to the concept of sin. The Rabbis feel that the eventuality of death entered the world as a result of Adam's sin, yet they do not, as Paul does, conceive of an "original sin" which is cast upon all those who follow Adam.[27]

There is no doubt that for Paul, who was so concerned with sin, death, and redemption, Adam is among the most significant personages of the Bible. His importance was so great that, as A. H. McNeile speculates, "the parallel drawn by St. Paul between Adam and Christ may have been the origin of the tradition that Adam was buried under Golgotha."[28]

Eve[1]

Other than the use of Eve in I Tim. as a basis for male supremacy, Eve is an important symbol of the church. Because of the strong Adam-Christ typology, it is very easy to compare the relationship of the first husband and wife to the supreme marriage, that of Christ and the church. Tasker feels that the church as the bride of Christ is prefigured in II Cor. 2-3.[2] This same motif apparently underlies the description of the church's responsibility in Eph. 5:31, although Eve is not mentioned explicitly there.[3]

Jonah

Jonah appears in only one pericope of the New Testament, a section which is Jesus' response to a request from the Pharisees and Sadducees in Mt. 12:38ff,[1] (from the crowd in Lk. 11:29ff.) for a sign. Actually, within this same pericope, as it appears in Mk. 8:11ff., Jonah's name is not mentioned, but Jesus tells the Pharisees that "no sign will be given to this generation," a response similar to the one appearing in the other two Synoptic Gospels. In Matthew and Luke, Jesus says that only the "sign of Jonah" will be given. Following the request and answer in the Gospel According to Matthew is a description of Jonah's and Jesus' three day sojourns, while in the Gospel According to Luke we find an explanation that Jonah was a sign to the Ninevites.

Mark's use of the "sign" tradition comes in the context of an overall rejection of Jesus by the Jews. R. A. Edwards speculates that the addition of Jonah's name to the sign in the Q document is for christological purpose.[2] N. Perrin agreed that the sign of Jonah is one of the Q units used in the Gospels.[3] Edwards contends that Matthew adapts it to show the suffering and descent of Jesus, and to illustrate the resurrection and its power, while Luke uses the "sign of Jonah" to illustrate the earthly preaching of Jesus.[4]

Whether we accept Edwards' hypothesis or not, it is clear that Matthew and Luke use this section for different purposes. In Matthew, Jonah is referred to explicitly as the prophet Jonah, which, according to Edwards, connotes the idea of "suffering because of the obstinacy of the Jews in refusing as God's word any word which threatened their world."[5] His suffering is pictured as three days' captivity in the belly of the fish, a period of suffering that points to the three days in the passion of Jesus before he was resurrected. As Tyson indicates, Jonah's three days and nights in the belly of the fish is a sign that Jesus will be in the bowels of the earth for the same period of time.[6]

The theme of three days and nights is an important one in reference to the resurrection, appearing in Mk. 8:31, Mt. 16:21,

17:22-23, 20:17-19; Lk. 9:22f., 24:46f.,; Jn. 2:19; I Cor. 15:4. All of these citations may, in fact, be implicit references to Jonah and his sojourn in the fish. Although Edwards feels that the use of the phrase "three days and nights" in some places could be merely as an idiom similar to "a couple of days" as we use in English, in the above-mentioned cases, however, it should be understood as a reference to an exact correspondence between Jesus' and Jonah's sojourns in Sheol.[7]

J. W. Doeve suggests that the resurrection's association with the number three has its roots in the bible itself.[8] In Synagogal Midrash, Jonah is connected to Hosea 6:2, which presents three days as the lapse of time from death to revival and being raised up. This strong identification of resurrection with Jonah suggests the possibility that such an association was intended by the New Testament writers when they included Jonah in the Gospels. Jonah as well as Jesus had a suffering-resurrection connection, and both preached to Gentiles receptive to their message.

Thus, Matthew, in using the figure of Jonah, concentrates on the "fish" part of the story. The "sign of Jonah" is his three days spent in the belly of the fish and his return to life.[9] For Matthew, who shows fulfillment of Scripture in Jesus' life, this typology is appropriate; Jesus was the antitype of Jonah in his own death and resurrection.

It is possible that Luke associated the "sign" with Jonah to illustrate his message of universalism. One concern of the book of Jonah is the demonstration that the pagan Ninevites were as much a concern to God as were the Israelites. God's mercy goes beyond particularism, extending to all who recognize Him. From another point of view, Zlotowitz points out that the book of Jonah lends itself to anti-Christian polemic since it shows that there are many ways to salvation. Not just the Jews, but also the wicked Ninevites could find a road to God through repentance, contrary to the Christian belief that one can only be saved by accepting Jesus.[10]

From Luke's point of view, the Jews of the first century were wrong in rejecting Jesus, for even the wicked Ninevites recognized the truth as preached by Jonah. Those who refuse to accept Jesus are like those who were unwilling to recognize the greatness of other men of God, like Jonah. Luke, therefore, sees a marked contrast between the Ninevites and Jews. Instead of typology, we have a case of parallel situations, wherein the Ninevites respond by accepting, the Jews by rejecting.[11] The comparison rests in the relationship between the proclamations of Jesus and Jonah. Thus, for Luke, the "sign of Jonah" is to be identified as his preaching.

Yet, both Matthew and Luke seem to caution against an equating of Jesus and Jonah in this pericope. "Something greater than Jonah is here" (Mt. 12:41, Lk. 11:32). Once again, the Tanakhic personage is a foil to show the superiority of Jesus. Jesus is not superior by virtue of a longer stay in Sheol or a more glorious resurrection; he is greater because his message goes out to all mankind, not just to the people of Nineveh.[12]

There is one other pericope which, although it does not mention Jonah, strongly suggests that Jonah was in the mind of the writer. Mk. 4:35-40, Mt. 8:23-27, Lk. 8:22-25, tell of Jesus' calming the storm on the sea, and includes a statement that Jesus was asleep in the stern. It is highly reminiscent of Jonah on board ship on his way to Tarshish in Jonah 1:4ff. Thus, Jonah's influence as a Tanakhic personage in the New Testament is felt at least once explicitly and once implicitly.

Solomon[1]

Solomon's great reputation is noted in almost all twelve references to him in the New Testament. Two of the three Solomonic references in Acts (3:11 and 5:12) and the solo mention of him in the Gospel According to John (10:23) speak of the "portico of Solomon," which, according to May and Metzger, was on the east side of the Temple.[2] The other Acts reference (7:47) simply names Solomon as the builder of God's house.

In Mt. 12:42 and Lk. 11:31, Solomon is mentioned in the "Jonah pericope." Solomon is cited for his wisdom, which was so great that the Queen of the South came from "the ends of the earth" to hear him. In a similar fashion, the wicked Ninevites were anxious to accept the preaching of Jonah. However, just as there is something greater than Jonah in the person of Christ, so, too, there is something greater than Solomon here, as well. The writer is apparently astounded by the

Jews' obduracy in their rejection of Jesus.

In Mt. 6:29 and Lk. 12:27, Jesus tells his disciples to have faith in God, for God will provide for their food and clothing. As an example of God's grace, Jesus points out the lilies, who are clothed even better than the great king Solomon was. Here, too, Solomon's reputation as a great historic figure is recalled by the New Testament writers.

Joseph

His first mention in the New Testament is in Jn. 4:4, where he is recalled as the recipient of the field given to him by his father Jacob. In Acts 7, Stephen's speech also recalls Joseph as he appeared in the Exodus story. He was sold into slavery, was rescued and brought to Pharaoh, became a prominent figure in Egypt, and brought his father and brothers to live with him.

In Heb. 11, he is mentioned as part of another historical event, his death. He forecasts an Exodus from Egypt and prescribes what to do with him after his death. He, like Jacob, had faith in the future. A. T. Hanson suggests that the caring for the disposal of his bones indicates that Joseph had faith in future resurrection.[1]

There are two possible implicit effects of Joseph in the New Testament. It is perhaps more than coincidental that the father of Jesus is named Joseph. In the genealogy, Joseph, the father of Jesus, is the son of Jacob, just as in the patriarchal line. In addition, Jesus' father, Joseph, is obedient to angelic messages in dreams. He takes his family to Egypt, of all places. The Biblical Joseph, too, went down to Egypt. His reputation as a dreamer and interpreter of dreams needs no explanation.

One of the most popular identifications of Joseph in the Bible is as one who is rejected by his brothers and sold to the enemy. He later forgives them for what they did. Jesus, too, is rejected by the majority of the people and is sold by one of his apostles to the enemy. In Lk. 23:24, the words "Father, forgive them; for they know not what they do," could be an echo of Joseph's forgiving his brothers.

Melchizedek

Melchizedek appears only twice in Scripture: in Genesis and in Psalms. When Abraham successfully completes his battle against a neighboring king, Melchizedek comes out to meet the Jewish patriarch in a nearby valley. Melchizedek, the king of Salem and priest of God Most High, brings out bread and wine and blesses him, after which Abraham gives Melchizedek a tenth of the spoils.

In Psalms 110:4, the king, presumably David, is told, "you are a priest for ever after the order of Melchizedek." The writer of Hebrews, assuming the Psalm is addressed to Jesus, uses this quotation to serve as the essential link between Jesus and Melchizedek. (Heb. 5:5).

Because Melchizedek is mentioned only once in Genesis, a genealogy should not be expected, for there are scores of Biblical personages without such description. Nonetheless, the lack of ancestors or descendants of Melchizedek is an important point for the writer of Hebrews in the connection between Melchizedek and Jesus.

The writer of Hebrews employs a technique that is similar to the methodology of the Rabbis, who inject their interpretations of Biblical personages and events into the Jewish tradition. When examining a text that lacks details, the Rabbis supplement the narrative, as does the writer of Hebrews with regard to Melchizedek.

The writer of Hebrews assumes that, because there is no genealogy, Melchizedek had no mother or father (Heb. 7:3). It is possible that the genealogical traditions associated with Jesus were not familiar to the writer of Hebrews. The earliest Gospel, Mark, shows no evidence of a genealogical tradition. Thus, to the writer of Hebrews, Melchizedek and Jesus share this factor.

A. B. Davidson believes that Melchizedek's lack of genealogy should not be taken literally. The absence of parentage in the text could mean that in spite of the fact that he is unconnected with any family, he has still become a priest.[1] Although he was born with no social standing, Melchizedek was able, in T. L. Leishmann's opinion, to make it on his own, not relying on hereditary succession.[2] F. L. Horton suggests that the lack of genealogy also underscores the originality of this personage.[3]

The lack of descendants makes it possible to speak of the eternal duration of Melchizedek. The Christ, too, endures for all time. Since there are no successors to Melchizedek, and no dynastic kingship is founded in his name, Jesus is not actually in the line of the Melchizedek priesthood. Rather, "every feature of significance in Melchizedek's priesthood is recapitulated on a grander scale in Christ's priesthood,"[4] thus making it a purely typological relationship, whose nature is emphasized by the five references to Jesus as a priest "after the order of Melchizedek" (5:6, 5:10, 6:20, 7:11, 7:170). C. H. Dodd believes that the comparison of Jesus and Melchizedek is one of only two or three cases of allegory involving Tanakhic personages in the entire New Testament.[5]

In most typological comparisons, the New Testament personage or situation is said to be like the type found in Scripture. Melchizedek, however, is said to be like the Son of God of the New Testament, thereby reversing the usual type-antitype language.[6]

A. T. Hanson submits that Melchizedek actually was the pre-existent Christ: "The author to the Hebrews undoubtedly maintains that Melchizedek is greater than Abraham. Who then can he be but the Christ?"[7] Hanson believes that the writer of Hebrews does not have the courage actually to say this, for "it was too strong meat for his hearers."[8] If Hanson were correct, then there would be no reference to Melchizedek being like Jesus, for if he is like Jesus, then how could he be Jesus?

There is an inherent association of Jesus and Melchizedek in the locale of the Genesis story. F. L. Horton suggests that Salem, a city of which we have no contemporary traces, could very well have been Melchizedek's location.[9] There is, however, much evidence that leads many scholars to speculate that Salem, meaning peace, refers to Jerusalem, the city of peace. In Joshua 10:11, Adonaizedek, a name strikingly similar to Melchizedek, is king of Jerusalem, thereby suggesting that there possibly was a tradition associated with the naming of Jerusalem kings. In Ps. 76:3, Salem refers to Zion, an important part of Jerusalem, said by some to be the only part of Jerusalem actually taken by David. Ps. 110 associates Melchizedek with Zion. Finally, Zedek itself is an ancient name for Jerusalem.[10]

A. R. Johnson feels that the story is extremely important in spite of the fact that it could be a "myth designed to justify the pre-Israelite worship of Jerusalem in the eyes of those who were worshippers of Yahweh."[11] Thus, Melchizedek is made the priest of God Most High (El Elyon) to give him an Israelite association. Johnson further suggests that the idea of righteousness inherent in Melchizedek's name was early associated with Jerusalem, concluding that there is no reason to doubt that Salem is to be identified with Jerusalem.[12] In any case, the fact that Melchizedek is associated with Salem suggests the ideas of peace and righteousness, making it easy to connect him to Jesus for "both qualities are commonly attributed to Jesus in the New Testament."[13]

The fact that Melchizedek was both a king and a priest is perfectly in accord with early Canaanite tradition.[14] Associating Jesus with Psalm 110 combines his royal and priestly aspects. Originally, the association of the Davidic king in Psalm 110 may have been made to emphasize the warrior-king aspects of David's rule, for we know from the Amarna letters that Melchizedek could also have been a warrior-king, a type of figure current in that region.[15] However, because the Biblical tradition attaches no such significance to Melchizedek in that respect,[16] it is unlikely that the association of Jesus with Psalm 110 was done for the purpose of giving Jesus warrior-like qualities, either. Such a suggestion would be inconsistent with the view of Hebrews.

Although general scholarly opinion holds that Hebrews had no connection to the Qumran community, it is interesting to note that the Qumran sect believed in the coming of two messiahs, one priestly and one kingly.[17] Combining these two roles in Melchizedek, and later in Jesus, is appropriate for the purpose of fulfilling that expectation.

Melchizedek and Jesus are equated in Hebrews in order to illustrate the writer's major theme, that Jesus is superior to all, and consequently, that Christianity is superior to Judaism. By equating Melchizedek and Jesus, the writer can show that in any case where Melchizedek is superior to another Scriptural character, Jesus also holds that relation.

The fact that Melchizedek blesses Abraham provides the writer with a basis for contending that Melchizedek must be superior to

Abraham. Not only was Melchizedek greater than Abraham, but he was also greater than Levi, for Levi was "in the loins of his ancestor when Melchizedek met him"[18] This principle is exhibited as early as Genesis itself when Canaan is punished for something that Ham, his ancestor, did to his father, Noah. It is because Canaan was in the loins of his ancestor, Ham, that the punishment is meted out to him.[19]

Melchizedek's superiority to Abraham derives also from the apparent paying of a tithe by Abraham to him. Actually, the antecedent of the Hebrew word expressing the giving of tithes is not clear in Gen. 14. Horton suggests that it might just as well refer to Melchizedek's giving Abraham a tithe,[20] thinking that it is not so unreasonable that a local king would reward a warrior such as Abraham was in the Genesis story, especially if Abraham had defeated one of Melchizedek's enemies. But in that case, what would Melchizedek be tithing to give to Abraham? Fisher speaks for many scholars when he says that "Abraham gives a tithe of the spoils which he obtained as the result of fighting for his king."[21] The writer of Hebrews apparently believes that Melchizedek, by virtue of his priesthood, was the recipient and thus is superior to Abraham.

The very fact that another priesthood should arise points to the conclusion that the Levitical priesthood was insufficient, another illustration of Jesus' superiority to the Tanakhic personages. Chronologically, of course, Melchizedek is the first priest mentioned in Scripture, but when the writer of Hebrews shows Jesus to be "after the order of Melchizedek' the issue becomes clear. Jesus arises to offer a more perfect priesthood than they had already.

The essence of Melchizedek's priesthood is contrasted to that of the Levites:

TABLE V

The Priesthood of Melchizedek and of Levi

Melchizedek	Levi
Royal (he is king).	Non-royal.
Abiding (his death is not recorded).	Non abiding (each is mortal).
Unique (no successors).	New Members in each generation.

111

Melchizedek	Levi
Receives tithes by God's authority.	Receives tithes by law's authority.
Receives tithes from Abraham himself.	Receives tithes from Abraham's descendants.

The epitome of the relationship of their priesthoods is contained in Heb. 7:9-10, "One might even say that Levi himself, who receives tithes, paid tithes through Abraham, for he was still in the loins of his ancestor when Melchizedek met him"

Implicit in the introduction of a non-Levitical priesthood is the thought that the commandments issued and enforced by the Levites were merely temporary and no longer in effect. Symbolically, with the bringing on of a new priesthood, the old one becomes obsolete, like the old law which failed to fulfill God's plan.

Although the blessing of Abraham by Melchizedek and the receiving of tithes could be pointed to as priestly acts, the writer of Hebrews apparently misses an excellent opportunity to link Melchizedek to a very significant Christian priestly act. Some scholars have said that the bringing out of the bread and wine by Melchizedek is symbolic of the sacraments.[22] It is neither mentioned nor alluded to in Hebrews, perhaps because the writer was more interested in modeling Jesus after Melchizedek in terms of his order than his priestly acts. Davidson feels that the author did not see the bread and wine as anything more than an act of ordinary hospitality,[23] and nothing priestly about it.

In any case, the sacramental aspects of Melchizedek's action do not stand out as other aspects of the story do to help the writer of Hebrews illustrate his major theme. Melchizedek is a convenient figure with which to associate Jesus to prove to his readers that Jesus is superior to all creatures, including the many heroes of Scripture, and therefore, that Christianity is greater than Judaism.

Levi[1]

The only significant mention of Levi is found in Heb. 7:5, 9, wherein Levi is described as the head of the priesthood which has genealogical rights to take tithes from the Israelites. Jesus and Melchizedek do not have the right from law but do so because their authority is greater. Levi himself paid tithe to Melchizedek "through the loins of Abraham," and thus Levi becomes a foil to prove Jesus' superiority.

Aaron[1]

Of the five references to Aaron in the New Testament, three of them are, as W. T. Davison calls them, historical.[2] Lk. 1:5 says that Elizabeth (the mother of John the Baptist) was "of the daughters of Aaron": in other words, of a priestly line, for the priests of Israel were descended from Aaron.

Acts 7:40, part of Stephen's speech, recounts Israel's history, mentioning the golden calf incident. Aaron, of course, acts as the leader of the Israelites while Moses is on the mountain, and according to Stephen, offers no protest but consents to make their golden calf. Contrasted to the Rabbinical interpretation, wherein Aaron is said to have delayed and attempted to stop the people from this sin, Stephen paints Aaron in an unfavorable light.

The third historical reference is made in Heb. 9:4 to the rod of Aaron in a description of the earthly sanctuary. The writer of Hebrews describes the ark with the rod of Aaron (along with the urn of manna) placed inside of it. In Num. 17:1ff., Aaron's rod is singled out as it blossomed before the people. It is chosen to be placed "before" the ark, not within it. In spite of this discrepancy, the reason for its presence is to remind the Israelites of God's aid to them in the wilderness. This description of the earthly sanctuary is denigrated by the writer of Hebrews who refers to the activities performed in that sanctuary as being imposed only "until the time of reformation" (Heb. 9:10). Once Christ appears, this earthly sanctuary is "obsolete."

It is important to note that this rod of Aaron was intended to be a symbol of his priesthood, a significant notion to the writer of Hebrews. The two remaining citations of Aaron appear here in Hebrews and, in both cases, it is Aaron's priesthood that is the focus, for one of the major themes of Hebrews is Jesus' high priesthood, of which office Aaron was the first to hold.[3] However, Jesus is not descended from Aaron, nor is he considered "a second Aaron." The typology, if there is any, is found in their divine appointment, the only attribute that they share.

Indeed, Heb. 7:11 points out the sharp contrast between Jesus and Aaron. Jesus is not part of that inferior priestly line of Aaron, but is "after the order of Melchizedek," an entirely different priestly order. Aaron's priesthood failed. Why else, according to Hebrews, would there be a need for another priest, Jesus, to arise?

The contrasts between the two are succinctly described by Davison: Jesus' priesthood is not "according to the Law"; Jesus is descended from Judah, not from Levi; none of the sacrifices of the Law could create perfection; and most important of all, Christ's priesthood is eternal, while Aaron's is temporary, becoming obsolete when Jesus appears.[4]

Noah (and Lot)

Of the eight mentions of Noah in the New Testament, not one of them occurs in Pauline literature. Barrett believes that Noah is not important to Paul, for "he stands between the two (Adam and Abraham) as an ultimately irrelevant figure."[1] Noah could have been significant as the connecting figure between the near extinction of mankind and the new start that was granted to man by God. In fact, Gen. 10 establishes Noah as the new head of the human race, which would seem to be an excellent opportunity for Paul to use as a type for Jesus. Yet Paul refuses to make the identification because Noah had commandments and laws associated with him. Paul's antinomianism leads him to choose Adam, not Noah. His mention in the Gospel According to Luke is merely as part of the genealogy leading to Adam.

Noah is a type in Mt. 24:37 f., Lk. 17:26f., and II Pet. 2:5 signifying the catastrophe that will come with the judgment of God. The use of Noah conjures up notions of a world destroyed by a deluge, an image important to the coming of the Son of Man. Similarly, in II Pet. 2:5, Noah is an example of the destruction that will come to mankind.[2]

114

In Heb. II, Noah is part of the "roll call." In the Bible, Noah is rewarded very clearly because he is a righteous man. The writer of Hebrews intends to show Noah as meriting his fate because of his faith. Righteousness was the judgment of God upon Noah, in return for the faith which pleased God.[3]

In I Pet. 3:20f., we find a double typology. The flood itself is a type for the baptism, for it was through the flood that the world was saved (as well as destroyed). Baptism, too, saves people by what it represents. The water of the flood, as well as the water of the baptism, directs people's conscience to God. Those who survived the flood are paralleled by those who are baptized into Christianity.

Noah is a symbol of the time of the flood as well as the leader to whom the people turn for salvation. Jesus is the symbol of the time of baptism, as well as the leader to whom the people turn for salvation. Just as Noah preached to his wicked compatriots, Jesus preached to imprisoned spirits.[4]

Pharaoh

In Acts 7, Stephen's speech includes the Egyptian king as he appears in the Biblical account: He recognized Joseph's wisdom (7:10), he became aware that Joseph's family was joining him in Egypt (7:13), and his (the new Pharaoh's) daughter rescued Moses from the river (7:21). The daughter of Pharaoh is also mentioned in Heb. 11:24 to help illustrate Moses' faith in rejecting his royal association to join his brethren.

In Rom. 9:17, Pharaoh is recalled as a tool of God for the display of His power to the people of Egypt. God deliberately hardens Pharaoh's heart to carry out the plagues against the Egyptians.

Abel (and Cain)

Abel's "fame" as the first person murdered in the Bible is the main reason he appears in New Testament writing. In the Gospels, Matthew and Luke use Abel as the terminus ad quo and Zechariah as the terminus ad quem[1] in the merism: "From the blood of Abel to the blood of Zechariah" (Mt. 23:35, Lk. 11:51), indicating that the Israelites are responsible for an enormous amount of innocent bloodshed, blaming even the death of Abel on the scribes and Pharisees. Abel is used as a chronological pinpointer, saying, in effect, that there has been innocent bloodshed from the beginning of time.

In Heb. 12:24, Abel's death is also recalled but, in this case, the blood of Abel is compared to the blood of Jesus. Abel's blood, in Gen. 4:10, cried out from the ground, apparently for vindication.[2] When his blood is mentioned in Heb. 12:24, however, it cries out for vengeance, while Jesus' blood, by contrast, cries out for man's forgiveness.[3] Once again, the Tanakhic personage's role is to place a value judgment on the relative merit of Jesus. According to J. H. Davies, the comparison here is that Jesus' blood signifies obedience, redemption, and salvation, while Abel's blood carries with it connotations of rebellion, hatred, and sin.[4]

The reason for Abel's murder was Cain's jealousy over the acceptance of his brother's offering more readily than his own, an event that is also mentioned in the New Testament.[5] Heading the list of examples of faith in the roll call of heroes in Heb. 11, Abel's offering to God is pointed out. The act of giving the gift was not as important as the faith behind it. It is this faith, in fact, through which, the writer of Hebrews says, Abel is still speaking.

Zechariah

Mt. 23 (Lk. 11) contains a discourse against the Pharisees in which Jesus says, "that upon you may come all the righteous blood shed on earth, from the blood of innocent Abel to the blood of Zechariah, the son of Barachiah, whom you murdered between the sanctuary and the altar." According to S. Blank, the phrase could be replaced with "throughout the course of your entire history, from the first instance of the spilling of innocent blood to the last."[1] Abel was, of course, murdered by his vengeful brother, Cain, as they stood together in the field. Zechariah of Second Chronicles was a priest who, after chastising the Jerusalemites, was stoned to death in the court of the Temple. There seems to be much evidence for matching the Zechariah of Mt. 23 with the Zechariah of II Chronicles. The

New Testament statement is a merism, sweeping the time span from the first to the last murder. Chronologically, Abel stands at the beginning, Zechariah at the end of the time span of Biblical history. In the Hebrew canon, Genesis is the first book, II Chronicles is the last. Thus, the Matthean statement mentions a murder at the beginning of the first book and at the end of the last. Blank cites Rabbinic tradition which describes the blood of Zechariah "crying out from the ground,"[2] a phrase highly reminiscent of that associated with the blood of Abel. The location in II Chronicles of Zechariah's murder is the courtyard of the Temple. The New Testament Zechariah is murdered "between the sanctuary and the altar."

Several problems, however, attend this explanation. The assumption would have to be made that the author of the New Testament tradition linking Abel and Zechariah used a Hebrew canon or some other arrangement of the Bible with II Chronicles at its close. We are unsure what Biblical orders were available then.

The order of the Jewish Bible preserved by the church as we have it today would lead us to believe that the New Testament was referring to Zechariah, the prophet, who gives his name to a Biblical book. Zechariah, in this arrangement of the Bible, is followed only by the book of Malachi. If the meaning of the phrase "from Abel to Zechariah" is to be interpreted as "from the first to the last," then a Biblical sequence extending from Genesis to a conclusion with the Minor Prophets would be consistent with that understanding. There is, however, no record of the prophet's death.

Another reason for identifying the New Testament Zechariah with the Biblical prophet is Matthew's mention of Zechariah's parentage, "the son of Barachiah." While the priest of II Chronicles is the son of Jehoida, the prophet is known by the identification as "son of Barachiah." The Gospel of Luke, on the other hand, includes no ancestry for Zechariah.

One possible explanation is that Matthew and Luke received this tradition from a common source with or without the name Barachiah. If the name was included, then Matthew could have failed to notice the problem and merely retained it in his Gospel. Luke, then, evidently unsure which Zechariah was intended, removed that part of the phrase from his version. If Barachiah was not included in the original tradition, then Matthew, for some reason, added it to his Gospel. If he assumed the Zechariah in II Chronicles was the intended referent, then he erred in identifying Barachiah as his father. If Matthew had access only to the LXX, he would not have known that there was another Zechariah for the II Chronicles personage is there called Azariah! In all likelihood, however, other versions of the Bible may have been available to Matthew, and we cannot know the readings there.

The other possibilities are that Matthew is the primary source and Luke read Matthew; or that Luke is the primary source and Matthew read Luke. In either case, the reasons for the removal or addition of Barachiah's name remain conjectural.

There remains the possibility that there was no confusion of Tanakhic personages at all, that the Zechariah to whom the New Testament refers is not even a Tanakhic personage.

In Josephus, Wars IV. v. 4, (Loeb: IV, 335-344), there is a Zecharias, the son of Baruch (the son of Baris) who is murdered by the Jewish zealots at the time of the revolt and was therefore probably a contemporary of the writers of the Gospels. He was slain in the "middle of the temple," after being declared innocent by the council of seventy judges. It is likely that this is the Zechariah to whom the New Testament refers.

While the Zechariah of II Chronicles incurred the wrath of the crowd by reprimanding them, this Zechariah was the victim of innocent bloodshed, like his counterpart in the Gospels. His death occurred in the Temple, very likely, "between the sanctuary and the altar." The identification by Matthew of "the son of Barachiah" is strikingly similar to Whiston's translation of Josephus' "son of Baruch." Baruch and Barachiah are, in fact, identical names in Hebrew. Even with Thackeray's contention that Baris is the proper reading, Matthew may have mistaken the name. All three writers, Luke, Matthew, and Josephus, could have had access to the news of this seemingly famous murder. Zecharias was "one of the most eminent of the citizens."[3] In reporting the incident, Luke could have felt that there was no reason to identify the lineage of Zecharias. Everyone would know to whom he was referring. All this is, of course, only speculative.

Thackeray dismisses such an identification of the New Testament Zechariah with that of Josephus. He claims that the entire proposal is based on "a rather remote resemblance of names."[4] We maintain that it was more than a "remote" resemblance. He also insists that the Zechariah of the Gospels is the Zechariah of II Chronicles, which leaves Thackeray with the problems already outlined. He feels that Matthew, "like some Jewish rabbis," confused the two Zechariahs. There is little evidence that such a confusion on the part of the Rabbis ever took place.[5] Thackeray, in fact, gives none.

Whiston is also confounded by the various Zechariahs. He contends that the Zechariah to whom Matthew refers is Zechariah the prophet. He had understood the words of Matthew "son of Barachiah" to be an intentional identification with the prophet of the Bible. Whiston also points out the problem that the Zecharias in Josephus was murdered after the death of Jesus and therefore could not be included in this words to the Pharisees. Yet those words could have been placed in the mouth of Jesus by the writers of the Gospels, who certainly could have been aware of this Zecharias' murder. That type of prediction would be quite appropriate in any of the Gospels where Jesus speaks often of future events. The context of this very pericope is a prediction by Jesus that he will send "prophets and wise men and scribes, some of whom you will kill and crucify. . ."

Accordingly, we contend that the Zecharias mentioned by Josephus is the most likely candidate. Jesus is alleging the Pharisees' responsibility for innocent bloodshed from the very first murder in recorded history, in essence, from the beginning of time; the most appropriate "Zechariah", therefore, should be the most recent from the perspective of the Evangelists.

The history of the Jews did not cease with the death of the prophet Zechariah or the priest Zechariah. Nor did the Jews' responsibility for innocent bloodshed, in the eyes of the New Testament, stop there either. Their responsibility continued to the present day, including the death of Jesus himself through the time of the revolt, to the most recent death they and their readers would recall, that of Zecharias. Jesus' statement, "from the blood of Abel to that of Zechariah" spanned the time from the beginning of the world's creation to its imminent destruction. Luke speaks of blood "shed from the foundation of the world [that] may be required of this generation." Accordingly, the New Testament writers were not using a Tanakhic personage other than Abel in this reference.

Judah (and Ahithophel)

Judah appears in both Synoptic genealogies. In fact, in Luke, there are two Judahs, one of whom is Judah, the son of Jacob, of Biblical history. In Matthew, Judah is singled out only because it is through him that Ruth is descended, and she, of course, is the ancestress of David, a racial link that has already been shown to be of great importance to Matthew.[1]

In Heb. 7:14, Jesus is also traced to Judah's line to show that Christ had no genealogical claim to the priesthood. Jesus overcame his "low non-priestly status" to become an exceptional priest like Melchizedek.

M. Enslin suggests a theory which traces the development of the Judas story throughout the Gospels beginning with the Markan narrative where Judas is mentioned only twice. Later, the story is embellished by Matthew and then Luke adds even more. Enslin believes that these embellishments are not historical but derive from the influence of certain Biblical characters.

Enslin suggests that Judah's influence is implicitly quite strong. He feels that the name of Judas was chosen as the betrayer of Christ precisely because of the association with Judah of the Bible. Their names are identical in Greek. "The very name Judas . . . and his position as one of the twelve, selling his master for money, is scarcely accidental, but would seem a clear reflection of the act of the earlier Judah. . ., one of the twelve brothers, urging the selling of Joseph to the Ishmaelites for twenty pieces of silver."[2]

Enslin claims that the story of Ahithophel, a member of David's council, committing suicide (II Sam. 17:23) is a source for a Matthean embellishment.[3] In a parallel act, Judas, a member of Jesus' "council," kills himself after finding out that his plans, like Ahithophel's, had not worked out.[4]

Enoch

Enoch is found in the Lukan genealogy, but without any special significance. Naturally, the Matthean genealogy does not include Enoch, for it extends only as far back in time as Abraham.

Enoch appears in Jude 1:14, where he is identified as being seven generations from Adam. The apocryphal book named for Enoch is quoted from in this reference.

Finally, Enoch appears in the "roll call" of faithful heroes in Heb. 11, where his faith is assumed. As J. H. Davies points out, Enoch must have had faith, for why else would God be so pleased with him that He would take him to heaven without causing him first to die.[1]

Rahab

Rahab is a very popular figure in several Rabbinic works and Josephus. J. H. Davies feels that the writers of the New Testament who used Rahab (Hebrews and James) must have been familiar with these traditions.[1] That is not necessary, however, for even in the Biblical account, she is pictured in a very positive light. Although called a harlot, she is very hospitable to the two spies and, as a result, Israel succeeds in its occupation of the land. She is rewarded by being spared when the Israelites conquer the city.

In Hebrews, she is included in the "roll call" of the faithful, for her faith that she displayed by her friendly welcome of the spies. Davies claims that the inference should be made that it was her faith in the knowledge that God would guide the Israelites to victory over her city that merited her inclusion in the "roll call."[2]

In James 2:25, Rahab is cited as a Biblical character who is justified not just by faith, but also by works. Her justification comes through her actual deeds, the reception and protection of the messengers.

Samuel (and Saul)

In Acts 3:24, 13:20, Heb. 11:32, Samuel is pointed out as a prophet. According to Acts, he is the first prophet, and, in Hebrews, he is singled out by name with "the prophets." Indeed, Samuel is special, for one of his functions in the Bible is to anoint David as king of Israel, thus making him the "messiah" or anointed one.

In Acts 13, Samuel is cited in an historical account leading up to an explanation of how David became king. There, too, it is Samuel's relation to David that gives him significance.[1]

It has been suggested that the birth of Samuel is a model for the birth of John the Baptist as they both came after barrenness of the mothers and were both celebrated with poetic declarations by the mothers. The "Magnificat," (Lk. 1:46-55) Mary's song of joy and praise, is based, in fact, primarily on Hannah's prayer (I Sam. 2:1-10).[2] It is interesting that John the Baptist "anoints" Jesus, in a sense, when he baptizes him, a point at which some believe Jesus became the messiah.

Joshua

Joshua is mentioned only twice in the entire New Testament. The first appearance is in Acts 7:45, where Joshua is used merely as a chronological pinpointer of when the Israelites first brought the tent of meeting into the land. From the time of Joshua until the days of David, the tent was with the Israelites.

The other mention is in Heb. 4:8, where Joshua is apparently berated for being a failure as a leader; he did not give the people "rest." In the Bible Joshua was understood to have finally brought the people to the land of Canaan, arriving at their home, achieving some "rest." They were the first generation to enter the promised land. The writer of Hebrews cautions against misunderstanding what "the rest" is. "The possession of Canaan was not the rest of God."[1] If it were "the rest," then why would God speak later of an unachieved "rest" in Ps. 95:11, where there is an implication that God has not yet allowed his people to enter "the rest"? Since the Psalms are understood to have dated from the time of David, and he chronologically follows Joshua, then Joshua could not have brought the people to "the rest."

Nevertheless, "Joshua' invasion is represented as a type of the rest into which the faithful in Christ would enter."[2] The remainder of Heb. 4 explains that indeed it is Christ who will lead the people to "the rest." There is apparently an ambiguous use of Joshua where, on the one hand, he has not achieved "the rest," while, on the other, he serves as an example of "the rest" to which Jesus leads.

An interesting play on words is present in Joshua's being eclipsed by Jesus. In Greek, Jesus' and Joshua's names are identical: "The verbal similarity suggests the similarity of the leader into Canaan and the leader into heaven, even while the sentence is stressing the difference."[3] J. H. Davies points out that the parallel of the names may not have been intentional but surely was noticed. If it was intended, then the writer preferred to not extend it, for this subtlety is barely developed.[4]

A. T. Hanson, however, chooses to develop it. The similarity of names is a hint that Joshua is not a type of Christ, but Jesus himself. Thus, Hanson says that Jesus is present with Israel in the dispossession of the nations of Canaan. The reason he did not grant them "the rest" was only because they rejected it along with him.[5]

Teeple points to three examples of Joshua's identification with the messiah: A church tradition reveals that a certain exalted man would come down from the sky and cause the sun to stand still (cf. Josh. 10:12); there was also a Jewish tradition that Joshua would return in messianic times; in Josephus (Ant. XX. viii. 6), there is an Egyptian Jew who claimed he would free Jerusalem from the Romans by making the walls fall down, an allusion making this"messianic redeemer" a new Joshua.[6]

An implicit identification of Jesus with Joshua is suggested in Heb. 2:10. In J. H. Davies' translation of the passage, the "leader who delivers them" alludes to Moses and Joshua as the type of leader that Jesus is.[7] As they led the Israelites to "the promised land", so Jesus will lead all mankind.

There are at least two other possible references to Joshua. In

Heb. 11:30, the fall of Jericho is cited as an example of faith in the roll call of Biblical heroes. Because the walls obviously couldn't be the antecedent, Joshua must be understood as the subject, the one who exhibited faith.

In Acts 6:6 and Tim. 4:14, the process of laying on of the hands as a sign of "ordination" of the disciples is mentioned, possibly alluding to the famous laying on of the hands by Moses when Joshua is selected as his successor in Num. 27:21-23.

Jeremiah

There are three explicit mentions of Jeremiah, but only as a source of a quote and not as a character. However, in Gal. 1:15-16, Paul describes himself as being set apart and called upon before he was born, words that are extremely reminiscent of Jer. 1:5, wherein Jeremiah describes himself in similar fashion. It is possible that Paul was modeling his mission after that of Jeremiah, both of whom preached to reluctant audiences.

There are at least two things about Jeremiah that would probably make Paul favorably disposed toward such an identification. Jeremiah, in 31:31-33, set forth the concept of a new covenant. According to Tyson, Jeremiah was one of the outstanding figures who looked forward to the restoration of the Davidic line.[1]

Esther

When Esther enters Antiochus' court to ask for a personal favor, she fears for her life. Such an intrusion into the king's presence without his invitation often resulted in death. However, Esther is received graciously by Antiochus, who tells her "What is your request? It shall be given you, even to the half of my kingdom." These words are echoed in Mk. 6:22-23, when Herodias' daughter, a young maiden as was Esther, is told by King Herod, "Ask me for whatever you wish, and I will grant it. . . whatever you ask me, I will give you, even half of my kingdom."

Miscellaneous

In the "roll call" of the faithful heroes of Heb. 11, there are numerous Biblical personages, some of whom are Gideon, Barak, Samson, and Jephthah, who appear only here in the New Testament. J. H. Davies feels that several other Biblical personages are implicitly referred to in Heb. 11:34ff.: Shadrach, Meshach, Abednego, the Maccabees, Elijah, Hannah, and Jeremiah, to name a few.[1] In all of these cases the Biblical personages are mentioned or alluded to as examples of faith, for it is the purpose of the writer to the Hebrews to show that the greatness of all of these characters is found in their faith. Davies thinks that the roll call is partially based on the same type of list found in Ecclesiasticus 44-50.[2]

Chapter III Notes

Moses

[1]T. Francis Glasson, <u>Moses in the Fourth Gospel</u>, p. 23.

[2]Howard M. Teeple, <u>The Mosaic Eschatological Prophet</u>, p. 75.

[3]<u>Ibid</u>.

[4]<u>R. S. V. Oxford Bible</u>, p. 1097.

[5]Ellis, <u>op. cit.</u>, p. 132; in Scripture, Moses organized the Israelites according to the tribes, numbering twelve. Jesus' disciples, also numbering twelve, are instructed to go to the Israelites and minister to them. Moses ascends a mountain to receive the law from God. When Jesus dictates the law to his followers, he, too, stands on elevated land: hence, the term "sermon on the mount." Moses performed ten plagues. Jesus performed ten miracles (See <u>infra</u>. p. 60). Moses provides food in the wilderness. Jesus feeds the multitude with loaves and fishes.

[6]Joseph B. Tyson, <u>A Study of Early Christianity</u>, p. 202; When Moses ascends Mt. Sinai, a cloud covered it for six days, giving the appearance of a fire on the mountain. In the transfiguration, a bright cloud overshadows Jesus on the mountain.

[7]Gundry, <u>op. cit.</u>, p. 209; when Moses "sealed" the covenant, it was with the blood of sheep or cattle. Jesus gives his disciples the blood of the covenant at the last supper.

[8]Spivey and Smith, <u>op. cit.</u>, pp. 115-121.

[9]<u>Ibid</u>.

[10]Teeple, <u>op. cit.</u>, p. 83.

[11]R. F. Johnson, "Moses," <u>Interpreter's Dictionary of the Bible</u> (hereafter cited as <u>IDB</u>), Vol. 3, p. 449.

[12]Spivey and Smith, <u>op. cit.</u>, p. 126.

[13]Tyson, <u>op. cit.</u>, p. 367.

[14]Teeple, <u>op. cit.</u>, p. 80.

[15]I. Renov, "The Seat of Moses," <u>Israel Exploration Journal</u> 5 (1955): 265.

[16]See also Mk. 12:39, Lk. 11:43, 20:46.

[17]Renov, op. cit., p. 262.

[18]Ibid., p. 266, quoting M. Ginsburger, "La 'chaire de Moise'," Revue des études juives 90 (1931): 161-165.

[19]A phrase pronounced by the rabbi as part of a Jewish wedding ceremony.

[20]Tepfer's theory was explained in an oral communication with H. C. Brichto, professor of Bible, Hebrew Union College-Jewish Institute of Religion, Cincinnati, Fall 1976.

[21]Spivey and Smith, op. cit., p. 212.

[22]Wayne A. Meeks, The Prophet-King, p. 292.

[23]C. K. Barrett, From First Adam to Last, p. 47.

[24]A. T. Hanson, op. cit., p. 54.

[25]Barrett, op. cit., p. 61.

[26]J. H. Davies, A Letter to the Hebrews, p. 48.

[27]Although Moses is thought of as the author of the Pentateuch, the New Testament makes it clear that the law of Moses is so-named only because God gave it through him. In Jn. 7:19, we seemingly have a departure from this principle. It appears that the law is attributed to Moses himself. Meeks suggests that this should be read as a statement, "Moses did not give..." similar to the statement in Jn. 6:32. The result would be strikingly parallel to Jn. 7:22-23, which immediately follows the statement in question, thereby supporting the principle which regards Moses as the vehicle through which the law is given (Meeks, op. cit., p. 287-288).

[28]A. H. McNeile, "Moses," Dictionary of Christ and the Gospels (hereafter cited as Dictionary of Christ), Vol. 2, p. 203.

[29]Meeks, op. cit., p. 287.

[30]A. T. Hanson, op. cit., p. 13.

[31] Meeks, op. cit., pp. 290-291.

[32]Glasson, op. cit., p. 25; see also Meeks, op. cit., p. 300-301.

[33]Glasson, op. cit., pp. 25-26.

[34]A. T. Hanson, op. cit., p. 111.

[35]Ibid., p. 75.

[36]A. J. Reines, professor of philosophy, Hebrew Union College-Jewish Institute of Religion, Cincinnati, class lecture, 10/29/75.

[37]Gundry, op. cit., p. 206.

[38]Teeple, op. cit., p. 1.

[39]Tyson, op. cit., p. 110.

[40]Ibid., p. 314.

[41]Teeple, op. cit., p. 47.

[42]Glasson, op. cit., p. 20; see also Teeple, op. cit., pp. 63-64.

[43]Teeple, op. cit., p. 74.

[44]Ibid., p. 83.

[45]Ibid., p. 86.

[46]Ibid.

[47]Meeks, op. cit., p. 294.

[48]Ibid., p. 290.

[49]Spivey and Smith, op. cit., p. 441; see also Meeks, op. cit., p. 318-319; see also Teeple, op. cit., p. 96.

[50]A. T. Hanson, op. cit., p. 117.

[51]Barrett, op. cit., p. 50.

[52]Tasker, op. cit., p. 32.

[53]Glasson, op. cit., p. 19.

[54]Spivey and Smith, op. cit., p. 447.

[55]Teeple, op. cit., p. 86.

[56]Glasson, op. cit., p. 21.

[57]Tyson, op. cit., p. 281.

[58]Ibid., p. 96.

[59]R. S. V. Bible, p. 1446.

[60]Shires, op. cit., p. 63.

[61]Teeple, op. cit., p. 93.

[62]Tasker, op. cit., p. 129.

[63]J. H. Davies, op. cit., p. 124.

[64]Ibid., p. 35.

[65]Ibid., p. 79.

[66]Ibid., p. 90.

[67]Glasson, op. cit., p. 54.

[68]Teeple, op. cit., p. 83.

[69] Ibid., p. 82.

[70]Robert Houston Smith, "Exodus Typology in the Fourth Gospel," Journal of Biblical Literature 81 (1962): 334-335.

[71]Ibid., pp. 335-336.

[72]Ibid., p. 339.

[73]A. T. Hanson, op. cit., p. 177.

[74]Meeks, op. cit., pp. 291-292.

[75]D. M. Smith, op. cit., p. 56.

[76]Meeks, op. cit., pp. 291-292.

[77]R. H. Smith, op. cit., p. 331.

[78]Tyson, op. cit., p. 262, quoting Justin, First Apology 60.

[79]Kee, et. al., op. cit., p. 341.

[80]Meeks, op. cit., p. 291.

[81]A. T. Hanson, op. cit., p. 120.

[82]Teeple, op. cit., p. 108.

[83]Glasson, op. cit., p. 20.

[84]Meeks, op. cit., p. 29.

[85]Barrett, _op_. _cit_., p. 58.

[86]Teeple, _op_. _cit_., pp. 31ff.

[87]Ibid., p. 40.

[88]Ibid., pp. 65-66.

[89]Spivey and Smith, _op_. _cit_., pp. 121-122.

[90]Ibid.

[91]Teeple, _op_. _cit_., p. 119.

[92]A. J. Tos, _op_. _cit_., p. 95.

[93]Ibid., p. 96.

[94]Tasker, _op_. _cit_., p. 24.

[95]R. H. Smith, _op_. _cit_., pp. 341-342.

[96]J. H. Davies, _op_. _cit_., p. 38.

[97]Teeple, _op_. _cit_., pp. 75-76.

[98]Tos, _op_. _cit_., p. 93; the quotations are: Dt. 5:9, 6:16, 8:3.

[99]Spivey and Smith, _op_. _cit_., p. 87.

[100]Glasson, _op_. _cit_., p. 17.

[101]Meeks, _op_. _cit_., p. 297.

[102]Ibid., p. 286.

[103]Ibid., p. 297.

[104]Tasker, _op_. _cit_., p. 34.

[105]Teeple, _op_. _cit_., p. 44.

[106]Ibid., p. 45.

[107]R. F. Johnson, _op_. _cit_., p. 449.

[108]J. H. Davies, _op_. _cit_., p. 36.

[109]A. T. Hanson, _op_. _cit_., p. 51.

110Barrett, op. cit., p. 60.

111Glasson, op. cit., p. 85.

112Teeple, op. cit., p. 120; see also Num. 11:24.

113Meeks, op. cit., p. 312.

114Ibid.

115J. H. Davies, op. cit., p. 137.

116Bernard M. Zlotowitz, "The Torah and Haftarah Readings for the High Holy Days," Central Conference of American Rabbis Journal 91 (Fall 1975): 103.

117Barrett, op. cit., p. 69.

118Ibid., p. 53.

119A. T. Hanson, op. cit., p. 33.

120Ibid., p. 32.

121J. W. Doeve, Jewish Hermeneutics in the Synoptic Gospels and Acts, p. 99.

122Tasker, op. cit., p. 91.

123Spivey and Smith, op. cit., p. 292.

124A. T. Hanson, op. cit., p. 32.

125Ibid.

126Spivey and Smith, op. cit., p. 292.

127A. T. Hanson, op. cit., p. 74.

128J. H. Davies, op. cit., p. 113.

Abraham

1A. B. Davidson, The Epistle to the Hebrews, p. 71.

2Spivey and Smith, op. cit., p. 26.

3Supra, p. 7.

[4]Barrett, op. cit., p. 33.

[5]See Ellis, op. cit., pp. 70-73.

[6]Barrett, op. cit., p. 77.

[7]Shires, op. cit., p. 113.

[8]Tasker, op. cit., p. 148.

[9]Ibid., p. 128.

[10]Ellis, op. cit., p. 120.

[11]Barrett, op. cit., p. 35.

[12]J. H. Davies, op. cit., pp. 62-63.

[13]Davidson, op. cit., p. 223.

[14]Barrett, op. cit., p. 68.

[15]Spivey and Smith, op. cit., p. 354.

[16]L. Hicks, "Abraham," IDB, Vol. 1, p. 20.

[17]George B. Stevens, Theology of the New Testament, p. 82.

[18]A. S. Geden, "Abraham," Dictionary of Christ, Vol. 1, p. 9.

[19]Martin Rist, "The God of Abraham, Isaac, & Jacob: a Liturgical and Magical Formula," Journal of Biblical Literature 57 (1938): 301.

[20]Barrett, op. cit., p. 39.

[21]Ibid., p. 43.

[22]Norman Perrin, The New Testament: an Introduction, p. 110.

[23]James 2:21ff. appears to be a reaction to this Pauline doctrine. James says faith and works together count for righteousness, mentioning the Akedah as a prime example of Abraham's important works.

[24]A. T. Hanson, op. cit., p. 125.

[25]Lindars, op. cit., p. 227.

[26]A. T. Hanson, op. cit., p. 125, quoting Chrysostom, Homilae in Genesis Hom. XLVIII (Paris 1862).

[27]Ibid., p. 123.

[28]Tasker, op. cit., p. 64.

Sarah

[1]Not placed according to decreasing frequency, but following Abraham for topical purpose.

[2]J. H. Davies, op. cit., p. 109.

David

[1]John Sampey, "David," Dictionary of Christ, Vol. 1, p. 418.

[2]Matthew Black, "The Christological Use of the Old Testament in the New Testament, " New Testament Studies 18 (1971): 2-4.

[3]Sampey, op. cit., p. 418.

[4]Tyson, op. cit., p. 357.

[5]David L. Cooper, Messiah: His Historical Appearance, p. 20.

[6]Gundry, op. cit., p. 210; cf. I Chr. 18:1ff.

[7]Tyson, op. cit., p. 387.

[8]Ibid., p. 357.

[9]Doeve, op. cit., p. 175.

[10]Tyson, op. cit., p. 110.

[11]Spivey and Smith, op. cit., p. 9.

[12]Tyson, op. cit., p. 110.

[13]Ibid.

[14]Ibid., p. 313.

[15]Spivey and Smith, op. cit., p. 102.

[16]Glasson, op. cit., p. 31.

[17]Meeks, op. cit., pp. 17-18.

[18]See Ps. 78:70, Ezek. 37:24.

[19]Kee, et. al., op. cit., p. 345.

[20]J. F. Bethune-Baker, Early Traditions About Jesus, p. 79.

[21]Shires, op. cit., pp. 127-128.

[22]Infra, pp. 122f.

[23]A. T. Hanson, op. cit., p. 61.

[24]Tasker, op. cit., p. 113.

[25]Hugh Anderson, "The Old Testament in Mark's Gospel," The Use of the Old Testament in the New and Other Essays, p. 301.

[26]Tasker, op. cit., pp. 29-30.

Elijah (and Elisha)

[1]Teeple, op. cit., p. 48.

[2]John A. T. Robinson, "Elijah, John, and Jesus: an Essay in Detection," Twelve New Testament Studies, p. 36.

[3]It might be argued that Elijah was also a man of water because of his prayer for rain on Mt. Carmel, and thereby parallel John's baptismal water; infra, p. 90.

[4]Teeple, op. cit., pp. 5-6.

[5]Robinson, op. cit., p. 29.

[6]Tasker, op. cit., p. 52.

[7]Anderson, op. cit., p. 295.

[8]Teeple, op. cit., p. 9.

[9]Meeks, op. cit., p. 27.

[10]Morton S. Enslin, Christian Beginnings, pp. 150ff.

[11]Robinson, op. cit., p. 44.

[12]Teeple, op. cit., p. 9.

[13]Robinson, op. cit., p. 39.

[14]Glasson, op. cit., p. 28.

[15]Teeple, op. cit., pp. 8, 48.

[16]Meeks, op. cit., pp. 26-27.

[17]Spivey and Smith, op. cit., p. 102.

[18]Kee, et. al., op. cit., p. 301.

[19]Herbert Baumgard, "Similarities Between Jesus and Elijah-Elisha," unpublished sermon, p. 4.

[20]Ibid., p. 2.

[21]J. H. Davies claims that the healing miracles of Elijah and Elisha are implicitly referred to in Heb. 11:35, op. cit., p. 116.

[22]Lindars, op. cit., p. 275.

[23]A contrasting view of this incident occurs in Jas. 5:17, where there is nothing miraculous about Elijah's prayer for rain being answered. He is merely an example of a faithful servant of God from Biblical times whose prayer was heard. James, in explaining the efficacy of prayer, uses Elijah to show that anyone can pray and be heard.

[24]Tyson, op. cit., p. 110.

[25]Spivey and Smith, op. cit., p. 366.

Naaman

[1]Not placed according to decreasing frequency, but following Elijah for topical purpose.

[2]Kee, et. al., op. cit., p. 310.

Jacob (and Rebecca)

[1]Rebecca is mentioned in Rom. 9 as the mother of the twin brothers, Esau and Jacob: " She conceived children. . . by. . . Isaac."

[2]J. H. Davies, op. cit., p. 112.

136

Esau

[1]Not placed according to decreasing frequency, but following Jacob for topical purpose.

[2]J. H. Davies, op. cit., p. 124.

Isaac

[1]Supra, pp. 75f.

[2]Davidson, op. cit., p. 226.

[3]A. T. Hanson, op. cit., p. 177.

[4]Tasker, op. cit., pp. 102-103.

[5]Supra, pp. 70ff.

[6]R. P. C. Hanson, Allegory and Event, p. 80.

[7]Ibid., p. 82.

[8]Roy A. Rosenberg, "Jesus, Isaac, and the Suffering Servant," Journal of Biblical Literature, 84 (1965): 386.

[9]Supra, pp. 72f.

[10]Ellis, op. cit., p. 122.

[11]Hans Joachim Schoeps, "The Sacrifice of Isaac in Paul's Theology," Journal of Biblical Literature 65 (1946): 385-392; see also "Isaac," Dictionary of Christ, Vol. 1, p. 839.

[12]L. Hicks, "Isaac," IDB, Vol. 2, p. 731.

[13]Dating the Midrash is an extremely difficult task. While some can be said to be Tannaitic, and others later, the dating of most is questionable even when they are attributed to specific historical personages. We have no way of knowing if the association is genuine or if the first mention of a midrash marks the beginning of its oral tradition. Most likely, some midrashim were existent in oral form for centuries before they were written down. Some concepts which have traditionally been regarded as Rabbinic in origin have been shown to actually have Biblical roots. H. Brichto, for example, in "Kin, Cult, Land, and Afterlife - A Biblical Complex," Hebrew Union College Annual 44 (1973): 1-54, has unveiled many such traditions. The purpose of including the Rabbinic sources here is to show the extensive interplay of thematic material from the Binding of Isaac and the Crucifixion, further illuminating the absence of Isaac/Jesus typology in the N. T.

[14]Rosenberg, op. cit., p. 386.

[15]Ibid., p. 387.

[16]Shalom Spiegel, The Last Trial, pp. 8, 36, and passim.

[17]Ibid., p. 44.

[18]Schoeps, op. cit., p. 389.

[19]Spiegel, op. cit., p. 43.

[20]Zlotowitz, op. cit., p. 99.

[21]G. Vermes, Scripture and Tradition in Judaism, p. 204.

[22]Ibid., p. 223.

[23]Ibid., p. 222.

[24]Ibid., p. 220.

[25]Ibid., p. 206.

[26]Ibid., pp. 206-207.

[27]Ibid., p. 227.

[28]Ibid., p. 225.

[29]Schoeps, op. cit., p. 391.

[30]Ibid., p. 389, quoting Israel Lévi, "Le sacrifice d'Isaac et la Mort de Jesus," Revues des Etudes Juives 178 (1912): 177.

[31]Robin Scroggs, Response to Edward Goldman's paper.

[32]Ibid.

[33]Barrett, op. cit., p. 29.

[34]Spiegel, op. cit., pp. 9-12.

[35]Rosenberg, op. cit., p. 388.

Adam

[1]Robin Scroggs, The Last Adam, p. 14.

[2]Kee, et. al., op. cit., p. 304.

[3]A. H. McNeile, "Adam," Dictionary of Christ, Vol. 1, pp. 28-29.

[4]J. H. Davies, op. cit., p. 30.

[5]Ellis, op. cit., p. 125.

[6]Ibid., p. 129.

[7]D. M. Smith, op. cit., p. 37.

[8]The idea of an "adam" naturally underlies the Rabbinic concept that a person who takes the life of a human being has wiped out an entire world, for just as Adam fathered a world of people, so each person is capable of the same.

[9]Barrett, op. cit., pp. 19-20.

[10]W. D. Davies, Paul and Rabbinic Judaism, p. 57.

[11]Interestingly, there is a midrash which claims that there were many worlds created, each of which was destroyed, before the one headed by Adam. Jesus as the head of a new creation is a concept not entirely dissimilar from this Rabbinic notion; see also Ellis, op. cit., p. 65; Tasker, op. cit., p. 108.

[12]Scroggs, op. cit., p. 59.

[13]Barrett, op. cit., p. 72.

[14]Ibid., p. 72.

[15]Ellis, op. cit., p. 129.

[16]Stevens, op. cit., p. 352.

[17]M. D. Hooker, "Review: The Last Adam (Scroggs)," Journal of Theological Studies 19 (1968): 282.

[18]Barrett op. cit., p. 9.

[19]F. R. Tennant, The Sources of the Doctrines of the Fall and Original Sin, p. 251.

[20]Scroggs, The Last Adam, p. 15.

[21]Ibid., pp. 10, 91; see also Hooker, op. cit., p. 281.

[22]Many scholars regard Genesis Rabbah as one of the earliest Midrashic collections, much of which formed part of an oral tradition that predated the written collection and could therefore have been accessible to Paul.

[23]Genesis Rabbah 12:6 on Genesis 2:24.

[24]Stevens, op. cit., p. 350.

[25]Spivey and Smith, op. cit., p. 347.

[26]Scroggs, The Last Adam, p. 58.

[27]Ellis, op. cit., p. 60.

[28]A. H. McNeile, op. cit., p. 29.

Eve

[1]Not placed according to decreasing frequency, but following Adam for topical purpose.

[2]Tasker, op. cit., p. 108.

[3]Ellis, op. cit., p. 129.

Jonah

[1]Jonah's name also appears in Mt. 16:4 in a repetition of the same sentence which appears here. There does not seem to be any more additional significance to that mention.

[2]Richard A, Edwards, The Sign of Jonah, pp. 106-107.

[3]Perrin, op. cit., p. 75.

[4]Edwards, op. cit., pp. 106-107.

[5]Ibid., p. 98.

[6]Tyson, op. cit., p. 166.

[7]Edwards, op. cit., p. 99.

[8]Doeve, op. cit., p. 149.

[9]Edwards, op. cit., p. 98.

[10]Zlotowitz, op. cit., p. 102.

[11]A. T. Hanson, op. cit., p. 175.

[12]Tasker, op. cit., p. 27.

Solomon

[1]Not placed according to decreasing frequency, but following Jonah for topical purpose.

[2]R. S. V. Oxford Bible, p. 1320.

Joseph

[1]A. T. Hanson, op. cit., p. 177.

Melchizedek

[1]Davidson, op. cit., p. 131.

[2]Thomas Linton Leishman, The Interrelation of the Old and New Testaments, p. 261.

[3]Fred L. Horton, Jr., The Melchizedek Tradition, p. 160.

[4]Ibid., p. 161.

[5]Dodd, OT/New, p. 6.

[6]Horton, op. cit., p. 156; see also J. H. Davies, op. cit., p. 67.

[7]A. T. Hanson, op. cit., p. 70.

[8]Ibid., p. 71.

[9]Horton, op. cit., p. 38.

[10]Leishman, op. cit., p. 159.

[11]Aubrey R. Johnson, Sacral Kingship in Ancient Israel, p. 43.

[12]Ibid., p. 42.

[13]J. H. Davies, op. cit., p. 67.

[14]Loren R. Fisher, "Abraham and His Priest-King," Journal of Biblical Literature 81 (1962): 269.

[15]Horton, op. cit., pp. 51-52.

[16]Ibid., p. 53.

[17]J. H. Davies, op. cit., p. 53; see also Teeple, op. cit., p. 47.

[18]Heb. 7:10; see also J. H. Davies, op. cit., p. 68.

[19]Herbert C. Brichto, professor of Bible, Hebrew Union College-Jewish Institute of Religion, Cincinnati, Genesis class lecture, Fall, 1976.

[20]Horton, op. cit., p. 14.

[21]Fisher, op. cit., p. 269.

[22]Bruce, op. cit., p. 13.

[23]Davidson, op. cit., p. 133.

Levi

[1]Not placed according to decreasing frequency, but following Melchizedek for topical purpose.

Aaron

[1]Not placed according to decreasing frequency, but following Levi for topical purpose.

[2]W. T. Davison, "Aaron," Dictionary of Christ, Vol. 1, p. 1.

[3]J. H. Davies, op. cit., p. 52.

[4]W. T. Davison, op. cit., p. 1.

Noah (and Lot)

[1]Barrett, op. cit., p. 25; each of those two had a significant role, one as father of the human race, and the other as father of the "chosen people."

[2]In Lk. 17:28, 29, and II Pet. 2:7, the Biblical personage, Lot, is added as another example of the disaster that will soon come to the world as part of the eschatology. The writers are obviously using Lot to allude to the destruction of Sodom and Gomorrah.

[3]Davidson, op. cit., p. 222.

[4]R. P. C. Hanson, op. cit., p. 68.

Abel (and Cain)

[1]Infra, pp. 116f.

[2]R. S. V. Oxford Bible, p. 6.

[3]Ibid., p. 1465.

[4]J. H. Davies, op. cit., p. 128.

[5]All three of the New Testament references to Cain focus on his evil character, and therefore serve as negative examples. The Christian is urged to be unlike Cain.

Zechariah

[1]Sheldon Blank, "The Death of Zechariah in Rabbinic Literature," Hebrew Union College Annual 12-13 (1937-38): 331.

[2]Ibid., p. 337.

[3]Josephus, Wars IV., v., 4.

[4]Josephus: The Jewish War, III (LCL; Cambridge, Mass. : Harvard University Press, 1928): 99.

[5]An examination of H. L. Ginzberg's Legends of the Jews (New York: Jewish Publication Society, 1947) reveals that there are no legends of murder associated with the post-exilic prophet, Zechariah. That the Rabbis did not confuse the two Zechariahs was confirmed to us in an oral communication with Moshe Assis, faculty member, Department of Rabbinics, Hebrew Union College-Jewish Institute of Religion, Cincinnati, Winter, 1976.

Judah (and Ahithophel)

[1]Supra, p. 79.

[2]Morton S. Enslin, "How the Story Grew: Judas in Fact and Fiction," Festschrift to Honor F. Wilbur Gingrich, p. 141.

[3]Ibid., p. 136.

[4]Ibid., p. 141.

Enoch

[1]J. H. Davies, op. cit., p. 107.

Rahab

[1]J. H. Davies, op. cit., p. 114.

[2]Ibid.

Samuel (and Saul)

[1]Saul, in his only New Testament mention, is included with Samuel for the same purpose here.

[2]R. S. V. Oxford Bible, p. 1241.

Joshua

[1]Davidson, op. cit., p. 95.

[2]E. M. Good, "Joshua, Son of Nun," IDB, Vol. 2, p. 996.

[3]J. H. Davies, op. cit., p. 45.

[4]Ibid.

[5]A. T. Hanson, op. cit., p. 61.

[6]Teeple, op. cit., p. 11.

[7]J. H. Davies, op. cit., p. 30.

Jeremiah

[1]Tyson, op. cit., p. 110.

Miscellaneous

[1]J. H. Davies, op. cit., p. 116.

[2]Ibid., p. 106.

CHAPTER IV

Concluding Considerations: A Jewish Perspective On the Christian Use of Scripture

In concluding our study, we should evaluate our findings in Chapters II and III in the light of the considerations outlined in Chapter I. How do the references to Tanakhic personages contribute to the evidence of a relationship between the New Testament and Jewish Scripture? How does their role help us to understand what underlies that relationship? Is that role different from the role of Biblical quotations: Did Tanakhic personages appear in such aids as testimony books or in an established oral tradition?

Two additional issues are appropriate for consideration. As a result of our study, could we consider the New Testament "Rabbinic" in any way? Does the role of Tanakhic personages in the New Testament affect a Jewish understanding of the New Testament?

As we have seen, the theory of a relationship between the New Testament and Jewish Scripture really needs no further substantiation. A consideration of the 400 explicit citations, in addition to the numerous other implicit references to Tanakhic personages, convinces the reader of the integral place the Scripture occupied in the formulation of the New Testament.

Although not as predominant as the role of passages, the role of Tanakhic personages extends throughout the New Testament. If we were to underline all of the places where they are mentioned or alluded to, there would rarely be a series of pages that would escape our pencil marks. To put it another way, if we removed all of the pericopes which contain a reference to a Biblical character, the New Testament would be very difficult to comprehend, as it would be missing some of its crucially important sections.

On the other hand, we should caution against overspeculation, as was pointed out in Chapter I with regard to Biblical passages. In many situations, Tanakhic personages do not appear where they could have been employed as perfect illustrations and appropriate examples. There are also some pericopes which have mistakenly been considered references to Biblical characters. Nevertheless, the lists and observations in Chapters II and III make it clear that Tanakhic personages, because of their frequency and impact, are a significant enhancement of the relationship between New Testament writings and

Jewish Scriptures.

We have also seen that authority was the key underlying reason for the use of the Bible by New Testament writers, and their use of Tanakhic personages brought that sacred authority of the Holy Bible to their text. The historical awareness and concern of New Testament writers for the fulfillment of Scriptural prophecy was also illustrated by the use of Biblical characters, some of whom made those very prophecies. Bringing those characters alive and having them appear with those of the New Testament maintained the important continuity and secured the connection between the two "testaments." By definition, any sequel to an original production must contain some of the cast of its predecessor. "The Old Testament Returns" or "Son of the Old Testament" may sound like frivolous Hollywood titles, but, in essence, that is the message of the New Testament. The New Testament writers were making the Jewish Bible a Christian possession, incorporating Judaism's heroes into their own tradition.

For someone such as A. T. Hanson, it is only natural that the Biblical characters should appear in the New Testament. Since, according to Hanson, Jesus appeared with them in the Jewish Bible, their reciprocal appearance in "His Bible" should be expected.

Tanakhic personages were part of a repository of material available to the New Testament writers, the Bible. These skillful writers used them as a literary device, since many of these personages were "ready-made" examples of ideas and themes which the New Testament writers were trying to convey. These characters were probably well-known figures, easily recognizable to the readers.

Thus, both Tanakhic personages and citations of texts became integral forms for the appropriation of Jewish Scripture. While citations were used in some cases, in others a mere reference to a Tanakhic personage was sufficient. Dodd claims that the Biblical quotation pointed to a larger context. So, too, a mention of a Biblical character probably reminded the reader of one or many stories about that figure. The use of Tanakhic personages, in fact, had an advantage over the citation of texts, for the characters lent themselves to a "midrashic treatment," the creation of fanciful legends about them. It is certainly easier to create tales about a person than about a passage.

148

It has been suggested that there were testimony books which contained particular Biblical quotations and accompanying recommended Christian interpretations, or at least that there was an established oral tradition containing such passages and explanations. Because the Tanakhic personages are interpreted in such different ways in the various books of the New Testament, we believe it is improbable that such tradition or testimony book containing much detail with regard to personages could have predated the New Testament. As we have seen, certain personages were important to particular writers, while other personages who appear in more than one writing were there to symbolize different things. It seems more likely that the main criterion for the selection and application of any Tanakhic personage is the tendency of the particular New Testament writer.

Each New Testament writer focuses on certain aspects of personages and in the process, establishes a tradition that, no doubt, was accepted by the later developing church. In other words, if there are "Christian" ways of looking at Tankhic personages, they probably have their roots in the manner in which those personages were presented in the New Testament, not before.

Clearly, there are several Tanakhic personages such as Moses, Abraham, David, and Elijah whose significance is more notable than others. Perhaps each writer had a particularly favorite personage in mind. Paul seems to favor Adam; Matthew prefers Moses; the writer of Hebrews focuses on Melchizedek. The most important thing to consider are the reasons that they are selected, which have been suggested at length in Chapter III of this study.

It is quite tempting to label the New Testament writers "Rabbinic." They, like the Rabbis, used Biblical material for exegetical and theological purposes, focusing on various aspects of these characters. Their styles and hermeneutics have something in common with that of the Rabbis in that they share a concern to use Tanakhic personages to prove points and to illustrate their philosophy.

Yet it is quite misleading to call the New Testament "Rabbinic," an adjective that implies an influence of the Rabbis on the New

Testament material. The problems of dating the Rabbinic and New Testament material prevent us from knowing which material predates the other. We also cannot be sure of the location in which the various sections of the New Testament were written nor the language of some sections thereof, and thus cannot know the degree of accessibility to any oral traditions which they might have shared. Theoretically, it is just as possible that the Midrash was influenced by the New Testament writings, or that neither was influenced by the other.

There is a significant difference between the goals of the Rabbis and those of the New Testament writers. When the Rabbis created midrashim to explain problems in the text so that its perfection would be secured, they very often glorified the characters of the Bible to intensify the positive attitude toward Judaism and to solidify Jews in their faith. When the writers of the New Testament used the Bible, they did so to show that its perfection can only be secured by faith in the New Testament, and, therefore, they often denigrated the characters of the Bible in order to glorify Jesus instead and either convince non-Christians to accept Christianity or solidify Christians in their faith.

Furthermore, while the Midrash has its origins in homiletical use, very often the Rabbis engaged in expositional midrash, a verse by verse explanation of the text. Frequently, it appears that the Rabbis intended that their work be examined in a "school" situation, for their midrashim often require extensive study to be understood. Clearly, the institutions and individuals who compiled the Rabbinic literature directed their efforts to a scholastic audience, for each midrash contains precise citations (proof-texts) pointing to exact events and personages.

The New Testament writers and those who transmitted their texts, on the other hand, were writing for popular consumption. Frequently, a citation is incorrectly assigned to the wrong Biblical book, or credited by Scripture in general or to one of its three major divisions. When a Tanakhic personage appears, rarely does a proof-text accompany it. Rather, the writers of the New Testament seem to allude more often to a popular image of an event or personage. The people to whom the New Testament was being addressed may have heard of the personages, but probably knew little detail about them, other than what was in the New Testament and thus, the writers could create a tradition about those personages as they depicted them. This is not to say that the New Testament writers invented the details about a particular Tanakhic personage. Rather, the writer's selection of certain details could play an important role in how the reader will understand that character. The books of Matthew and Hebrews, which, more than others, may have been directed at a group of people with more background in Bible, do in fact contain more detail and more references to Tanakhic personages.

Another explanation of the similarities and differences between the New Testament and Rabbinic literature is that they both developed independently. Although their objectives were not the same, they were both working with the same material, the Bible, and, therefore, some of their conclusions were bound to be identical, thus giving an appearance that they were dependent on each other. The fact that ideas often develop simultaneously and independently does not detract from the originality and individuality of those responsible. So, too, here, the integrity of each tradition, Christian and Jewish, can be preserved.

The recognition of the integrity of the New Testament tradition could preclude the integrity of the Jewish tradition. One of the recurring uses of Tanakhic personages in the New Testament is to show that they are inferior to Jesus and to conclude that Christianity is superior to Judaism. If we accept A. T. Hanson's basic premise, that Jesus Christ was actually present in the Bible, then the idea of the Jews' rejection of Jesus becomes magnified. It is clear that one of the major themes of the New Testament is Jesus' rejection by the Jews of his day, who were obstinate in their refusal to accept his divinity. Hanson would have us believe that that obduracy is even deeper seated in history, for the Jews show their ignorance of Christ's presence even during their sojourn in Sinai.

It is no wonder that Jews in the twentieth century are not overly eager to study the New Testament, for they are both afraid and hesitant about such a venture. Approaches such as the one professed by A. T. Hanson can only further the chasm that exists between Jew and Christian.

By and large, neither Jew nor Christian understands the background and history out of which the New Testament was molded.

Instead, each regards the other's religion as either a monolith or amorphous mass.

One of the results of our study is the understanding that the New Testament is multifaceted, more an anthology than anything else, containing varying viewpoints and different approaches to key religious questions.

This study has hopefully added some understanding as to how our two traditions do overlap. We have shown that the Tanakhic personages are important to Christianity as well as to Judaism, albeit for different reasons. However, as a child whose parents are separated or divorced may be loved and cherished by both of those parents, so, too, a recognition that Jews and Christians hold things in common can also lead to a more healthy relationship between our communities of faith.

Bibliography

Anderson, Hugh. "The Old Testament in Mark's Gospel," The Use of the Old Testament in the New and Other Essays: Studies in Honor of William Franklin Stinespring. Edited by James M. Efird. Durham, N. C. : Duke University Press, 1972: 280-306.

Barrett, C. K. From First Adam to Last: A Study in Pauline Theology. New York: Charles Scribner's Sons, 1962.

Barth, Karl. Christ and Adam: Man and Humanity in Romans 5. Scottish Journal of Theology Occasional Papers, No. 5. Translated from the German by T. A. Smail. London: Oliver & Boyd, 1956.

Baumgard, Herbert M. "Similarities Between Jesus and Elijah-Elisha." Mimeographed Sermon. Miami, Florida: n.d.

Bethune-Baker, J[ames] F[ranklin]. Early Traditions About Jesus. New York: Macmillan Co., 1930.

Black, Matthew. "The Christological Use of the Old Testament in the New Testament," New Testament Studies 18 (1971): 1-14.

Blank, Sheldon H. "The Death of Zechariah in Rabbinic Literature," Hebrew Union College Annual 12-13 (1937-38): 327-346.

Bonus, Albert. "Jonah," James Hastings' A Dictionary of Christ and the Gospels (1911), Vol. 1: 895-897.

Brachman, Abraham J. "A Correlation of the Book of Mark with the Books of the Bible, Talmud, and Liturgy," Central Conference of American Rabbis Journal 22 (June 1958): 68-72.

Bruce, F. F. The New Testament Development of Old Testament Themes. Grand Rapids, Mich. : Wm. B. Eerdmans Co., 1968.

Childs, B. S. "Adam," Interpreter's Dictionary of the Bible (1962), Vol. 1: 43-44.

Cooper, David L. Messiah: His Historical Appearance. Abridged ed.

155

Los Angeles: Biblical Research Society, 1961.

Daniélou, Jean. From Shadows to Reality: Studies in the Biblical Typology of the Fathers. Translated from the French by Dom Wulstan Hibberd. London: Burns & Oates, 1960.

Davidson, A. B. The Epistle to the Hebrews. Grand Rapids, Mich. : Zondervan Publishing House, 1952.

Davies, J. H. A Letter to Hebrews. Cambridge: University Press, 1967.

Davies, W. D. Paul and Rabbinic Judaism: Some Rabbinic Elements in Pauline Theology. 2d Ed. with additional notes. London: S. P. C. K., 1965.

_____. Review of The New Testament and Rabbinic Judaism, by David Daube. New Testament Studies 3 (1957): 354-357.

Davison, W. T. "Aaron," James Hastings' A Dictionary of Christ and the Gospels (1911), Vol. 1:1.

Dodd, C[harles] H[arold]. According to the Scriptures: The Sub-Structure of New Testament Theology. London: Nisbet & Co., 1953.

_____. The Old Testament in the New. Revised. Facet Books Biblical Series 3. John Reumann, General Editor. Philadelphia: Fortress Press, 1971.

Doeve, J[an] W[illiam]. Jewish Hermeneutics in the Synoptic Gospels and Acts. Assen, Netherlands: Van Gorcum & Co. N.V., 1954.

Edwards, Richard A. The Sign of Jonah: In the Theology of the Evangelists and Q. Studies in Biblical Theology, Second Series, No. 18. Naperville, Ill. : Alec R. Allenson, n.d.

Ellis, E. Earle. Paul's Use of the Old Testament. Edinburgh: Oliver & Boyd, 1957.

Enslin, Morton Scott. Christian Beginnings. 3 vols. 1938. Reprint

(Vols. 1 & 2 in 1). New York: Harper & Row, Harper Torchbooks, 1956.

_____. "How the Story Grew: Judas in Fact and Fiction," Festschrift to Honor F. Wilbur Gingrich. Edited by Eugene Howard Barth and Ronald Edwin Cocroft. Leiden: E. J. Brill, 1972: 123-141.

Fisher, Loren R. "Abraham and His Priest-King," Journal of Biblical Literature 81 (1962): 264-270.

Gates, O. A. "Elijah," James Hastings' A Dictionary of Christ and the Gospels (1911), Vol. 1:514.

Geden, A. S. "Abraham," James Hastings' A Dictionary of Christ and the Gospels (1911), Vol. 1:8-9.

Glasson, T. Francis. Moses in the Fourth Gospel. Studies in Biblical Theology, No. 40. London: SCM Press, 1963.

Good, E. M. "Joshus, Son of Nun," Interpreter's Dictionary of the Bible, Vol. 2:995-996.

Gundry, Robert Horton. The Use of the Old Testament in St. Matthew's Gospel: With Special Reference to the Messianic Hope. Leiden: E. J. Brill, 1967.

Hanson, Anthony Tyrell. Jesus Christ in the Old Testament. London: SCM Press, 1959.

Harris, Rendel. Testimonies. Part 2. Cambridge: University Press, 1920.

Hastings, James, ed. A Dictionary of Christ and the Gospels. 2 vols. New York: Charles Scribner's Sons, 1911.

Hicks, L. "Abraham," Interpreter's Dictionary of the Bible (1962), Vol. 1:14-21.

_____. "Isaac," Interpreter's Dictionary of the Bible (1962), Vol. 2:728-731.

_____. "Melchizedek," Interpreter's Dictionary of the Bible (1962), Vol. 3:343.

Hooker, M. D. Review of The Last Adam, by Robin Scroggs. Journal of Theological Studies 19 (1968): 281-282.

Interpreter's Dictionary of the Bible: An Illustrated Encyclopedia. Ed. George Arthur Buttrick, et. al. 4 Vols. New York: Abingdon Press, 1962.

"Isaac," James Hastings' A Dictionary of Christ and the Gospels (1911), Vol. 1:839.

Johnson, A[ubrey] R. Sacral Kingship in Ancient Israel. Cardiff: University of Wales Press, 1955.

Johnson, R. F. "Moses," Interpreter's Dictionary of the Bible (1962), Vol. 3:440-450.

Josephus, Flavius. The Life and Works of Flavius Josephus. . . Translated from the Greek by William Whiston. New York: Holt, Rinehart & Winston, n.d.

Kee, Howard Clark; Young, Franklin W.; and Froehlich, Karlfried. Understanding the New Testament. 2d. ed. Englewood Cliffs, N.J.: Prentice-Hall, 1965.

Leishman, Thomas Linton. The Interrelation of the Old and New Testaments. New York: Vantage Press, 1968.

Lindars, Barnabas. New Testament Apologetic: The Doctrinal Significance of the Old Testament Quotations. Study ed. London: SCM Press, 1961.

Mauch, T. M. "Aaron," Interpreter's Dictionary of the Bible (1962), Vol. 1:1-2.

McNeile, A. H. "Adam," James Hastings' A Dictionary of Christ and the Gospels (1911), Vol. 1:28-29.

_____. "Moses," James Hastings' A Dictionary of Christ and

the Gospels (1911), Vol. 2:203-205.

Meeks, Wayne A. The Prophet-King: Moses Traditions and the Johannine Christology. Leiden: E. J. Brill, 1967.

Myers, J. M. "David," Interpreter's Dictionary of the Bible (1962), Vol. 1:771-782.

"Myth and the Gospel (Contd.), " Time March 17, 1961:51.

Neil, W. "Jonah, Book of," Interpreter's Dictionary of the Bible (1962), Vol. 2: 964-967.

Nelson's Complete Concordance of the Revised Standard Version Bible. Ed. John W. Ellison. New York: Thomas Nelson & Sons, 1957.

Oxford Annotated Bible with the Apocrypha; Revised Standard Version. Ed. by Herbert G. May and Bruce M. Metzger. College ed. New York: Oxford University Press, 1965.

Perrin, Norman. The New Testament, an Introduction: Proclamation and Parenesis, Myth and History. New York: Harcourt Brace Jovanovich, 1974.

Renov, I[srael]. "The Seat of Moses," Israel Exploration Journal 5 (1955):262-267.

Rist, Martin. "The God of Abraham, Isaac & Jacob: A Liturgical and Magical Formula," Journal of Biblical Literature 57 (1938): 289-303.

Robinson, John A. T. "Elijah, John, and Jesus, an Essay in Detection," from New Testament Studies 4 (1958):263-281. Reprinted in John A. T. Robinson. Twelve New Testament Studies. Studies in Biblical Theology. Naperville, Ill.: Alec R. Allenson, 1962.

Rosenberg, Roy A. "Jesus, Isaac, and the 'Suffering Servant'," Journal of Biblical Literature 84 (1965):381-388.

Sandmel, Samuel. A Jewish Understanding of the New Testament. Augmented ed. New York: KTAV, 1974.

Schoeps, Hans Joachim. "The Sacrifice of Isaac in Paul's Theology," Journal of Biblical Literature 65 (1946):385-392.

Scroggs, Robin. Response to Edward Goldman's paper "The Binding of Isaac in the Rabbinic Literature." Paper read at Centenniel Celebration in Honor of the Hebrew Union College, 15 May 1976, at University of Chicago Divinity School. Photocopied.

_____. The Last Adam: A Study in Pauline Anthropology. Oxford: Basil Blackwell, 1966.

Sempey, John R. "David," James Hastings' A Dictionary of Christ and the Gospels (1911), Vol. 1:417-418.

Shires, Henry M. Finding the Old Testament in the New. Philadelphia: Westminster Press, 1974.

Smith, D. Moody, Jr. "The Use of the Old Testament in the New," The Use of the Old Testament in the New and Other Essays: Studies in Honor of William Franklin Stinespring. Edited by James M. Efird. Durham, N. C.: Duke University Press, 1972.

Smith, Robert Houston. "Exodus Typoology in the Fourth Gospel," Journal of Biblical Literature 81 (1962): 329-342.

Spiegel, Shalom. The Last Trial: . . .the Akedah. Translated from the Hebrew by Judah Goldin. Philadelphia: Jewish Publication Society of America, 1967.

Spivey, Robert A. and Smith, D. Moody, Jr. Anatomy of the New Testament: A Guide to its Structure and Meaning. 2d. ed. New York: Macmillan Co., 1974.

Stevens, George Barker. The Theology of the New Testament. New York: Charles Scribner's Sons, 1905.

Szikszai, S. "Elijah, the Prophet," Interpreter's Dictionary of the Bible (1962), Vol. 2:89-90.

Tasker, R. V. G. The Old Testament in the New Testament. Philadelphia: Westminster Press, 1947.

Teeple, Howard M. The Mosaic Eschatological Prophet. Journal of Biblical Literature Monograph Series, Vol. 10. Philadelphia: Society of Biblical Literature, 1957.

Tennant, F. R. The Sources of the Doctrines of the Fall and Original Sin. New York: Schocken Books, 1968.

Thomas, W, H, Griffith. "Priest," James Hastings' A Dictionary of Christ and the Gospels (1911), Vol. 2:415-418.

Throcknorton, Burton H., Jr. Gospel Parallels: A Synopsis of the First Three Gospels. 3d. ed. rev. New York: Thomas Nelson, 1973.

Tos, Aldo J. Approaches to the Bible: The Old Testament. Englewood Cliffs, N.J.: Prentice-Hall, 1963.

Tyson, Joseph B. A Study of Early Christianity. New York: Macmillan Co., 1973.

Zlotowitz, Bernard M. "The Torah and Haftarah Readings for the High Holy Days," Central Conference of American Rabbis Journal 91 (Fall 1975):93-105.

About the author

Norman M. Cohen is the founding Rabbi and spiritual leader of Bet Shalom Congregation, located in Minneapolis, Minnesota.

Presently, in addition to his congregational duties, Rabbi Cohen is a faculty member at St. Olaf College in Northfield, and the United Theological Seminary in New Brighton, and has also taught at the College of St. Catherine in St. Paul, Edgecliff College, Xavier University and his alma mater, Hebrew Union College-Jewish Institute of Religion, in Cincinnati.

Rabbi Cohen received his bachelor's degree, cum laude, from Holy Cross College in Worcester, Massachusetts, in 1972. His studies included a six-month program in Jerusalem at the Hiatt Institute of Brandeis University. His graduate work was done at Hebrew Union College-Jewish Institute of Religion in Cincinnati, Ohio, where he received the degree of M.A.H.L. in 1975 and rabbinic ordination in 1977.